The 100X Life:

**7 Simple Daily Habits That Will Transform Your Life,
Unlock Your Greatest Potential, and
Create a Life Beyond Your Wildest Dreams!**

Stephen F. Skinner

D1378253

Published in the United States of America

Disclaimer:

The 100X Life offers health, fitness, and nutritional information and is for educational purposes only. This book is intended to supplement, not replace, the professional medical advice, diagnosis, or treatment of health conditions from a trained health professional. Please consult your physician or other healthcare professional before beginning or changing any health or fitness program to make sure that it is appropriate for your needs, especially if you are pregnant or have a family history of any medical concerns, illnesses, or risks. If you have any concerns or questions about your health, you should always consult with a physician or other healthcare professional. Stop exercising immediately if you experience faintness, dizziness, pain, or shortness of breath at any time. Please do not disregard, avoid, or delay obtaining medical or health-related advice from your healthcare professional because of something you may have read in this guide.

No part of this publication may be reproduced or transmitted in any form or by any means, mechanical or electronic, including photocopying or recording, or by any information storage and retrieval system, or transmitted by email without permission in writing from the publisher. While all attempts have been made to verify the information provided in this publication, neither the author nor the publisher assumes any responsibility for errors, omissions, or contrary interpretations of the subject matter herein. This book is for entertainment purposes only. The views expressed are those of the author alone, and should not be taken as expert instruction or commands. The reader is responsible for his or her own actions. Adherence to all applicable laws and regulations, including international, federal, state, and local laws governing professional licensing, business practices, advertising, and all other aspects of doing business in the US, Canada, or any other jurisdiction is the sole responsibility of the purchaser or reader. Neither the author nor the publisher assumes any responsibility or liability whatsoever on the behalf of the purchaser or reader of these materials. Any perceived slight of any individual or organization is purely unintentional.

Statements about products and health conditions have not been evaluated by the US Food and Drug Administration. Products and information presented herein are not intended to diagnose, treat, cure, or prevent disease. If you have any concerns about your own health, you should always consult with a physician or other healthcare professional. Your use of this book indicates your agreement.

Endorsements:

"Personal. Energizing. Life-changing. I love Stephen's approach to this challenge that we all have—How do we find enough margin to experience significant fulfillment in life and work? Stephen pulls back the curtain on his story of success and shows you how and why it all fell apart. He explains how he made it through this chaotic time and how his life and work changed forever. His simple, yet powerful step-by-step process will be life-changing for you!"

Mike Nichols
President, The Guidestone Group

"Stephen Skinner is the real deal. A man of high character with core values second to none. To say that he has had a life transformation is an understatement. With his new book, *The 100X Life*, he describes in great detail a process for anyone who wants to grow or transform their life and make a real difference in the families, careers, and even their community. Reading this book will be time well spent."

Aaron Walker
President & Founder, View from the Top

"I had the pleasure of meeting Stephen the Fall of 2014 after losing my son Philip as a passenger in a single vehicle accident. Stephen 'walks the walk' on daily bases by giving himself, his loving heart, passions, kindness and goodness to everyone he meets. Stephen lives the 7 intentional habits each and every day through his daily interactions with family, employees, friends and the charities he supports. Join Stephen on the journey of a more loving, giving, serving and fulfilling life by living with intent."

Mike Lutzenkirchen
Executive Director, Lutzie 43 Foundation

"I have known Stephen for a long time, and I have seen this transformation, firsthand. I highly recommend this for anyone who truly desires to grow/transform their life and make a difference."

Hank Apel
Vice President, Apel Steel

"I have watched Stephen mature and grow into the quality person that I now admire and respect."

Roger Humphrey

"I have known Stephen for many years and I can tell you, he is a changed man. I knew some of the reason for this transformation, but this simple step-by-step daily process explains so much! If you want to start living your life intentionally and not just 'existing' each day, this book is for you. I highly recommend this for anyone who wants to transform their life and make a difference. If you are ready to experience change for the better, this book is a must-read."

Natalie Drake
Business Owner, Long Term Care Facility & Marketing Consultant

"Stephen Skinner uses his time and talent to serve others. His book will teach you how to make a lasting impact through your legacy. Stephen will help you to chart a path by drawing on his own experiences that have transformed him into a different person. I highly recommend this book to anyone who wants to make a difference and transform their life. If you want to be a catalyst for change in your personal life, business, and community, then read this book!"

James Justice
President and Founder, Alliance of Marketplace Leaders

"I know Stephen, and I can tell you he now lives an intentional life. I am so glad he has shared his simple step-by-step daily process so others can experience the same transformation! I highly recommend this book for anyone who wants to maximize their impact in their family, business, or community!"

Chris J. Patton
ChristianFaithAtWork.com

"I have a great amount of respect for Stephen, both personally and professionally. His breakdown of these simple daily processes really puts things into perspective, and if utilized, can take your business to the next level. I highly recommend!"

Clay Colvard
President, Colvard Insurance Associates, Inc. Allstate Insurance

"Stephen's journey closely mirrors my own. I too had to hit a bottom. I have traveled a long way from where I was and made many changes, with the help of God and other people who have improved their family, spiritual and work lives. This book comes at a very important time for me, though . . . a time when I am in need of fine tuning and also at a time when I need to be careful to not rest on my laurels. This book helps those who are desperate for a change in their 'whole life' and also for those who have made major changes but are now looking for fine tuning in pursuing God's will for their life."

Wayne Herring
Founder, www.StrongerSalespeople.com

"Two words come to mind when I think of Stephen Skinner: Authentic & Authoritative. He's a man on a mission with a big heart to help people. If you ever get the chance to meet him, I'm sure you'll agree with me, he's the real deal. He lives what he writes. It's never just theory, but he always communicated practical truths that I can apply today to make a difference. I never miss a chance to read what he writes."

Dennis McIntee
Founder & CEO, The Leadership Process

"This is a great book! It delivers on its promise of the 7 daily habits that will change your life forever. Implementing these habits has made a huge difference in my life, and I'm sure they will take your life to the next level also."

Eric Gonia
Amazon.com Verified Purchase Reviewer

"Who doesn't need a 100x ROI? I looked at the title of this book and immediately jumped into the content. It is truly inspiring to hear/read the author's background and struggles he laid out at the beginning of the book. I instantly related on the grind and over working aspects. I find myself tired and exhausted trying to do it on my own.

But it was how the author laid out his steps to PLANT the seeds that really turned my head. As a former pastor, I am very familiar with this parable. However, I was convicted to read on the 'time to plant' aspect in the book. I usually keep myself up late at night, trying to fill in every last detail of work before I go to bed. This is a bad habit that needs to be changed. I loved the research and resources that the author shared to change this habit. The people he referenced and their impact in the world has truly flipped a switch. I need to change. I need to see my 100x ROI.

I am truly excited to apply some of *The 100x Life* principles to my own journey to see the transformation in my life and better yet, God's kingdom, the people.

You all need to read this book!!!"

Jared Buckley
Amazon.com Verified Purchase Reviewer

"Wow, this book really resonates because I was exactly where Stephen was eight years ago. It would have been great to have this book at that time . . . that would have been the best time to have this book . . . but, they say the second best time is always now . . . so I am glad to have this book to refer to as I go forward. For me this book will be about fine tuning and staying mentally, physically and spiritually fit. I have written down three habits that I plan to incorporate into my daily routine. This book is a must-read for those looking to maximize their positive impact on their families, businesses, and communities."

Anonymous
Amazon.com Verified Purchase Reviewer

YOUR FREE GIFTS

As a way of saying thanks for your purchase, we're offering free gifts throughout, which are exclusive to our book readers.

First, I would like to invite you to join *The 100X Life Community on Facebook*, which is a group made up of other highly motivated, inspired, and like-minded individuals who support each other every day. I hope to see you there! When you get there, please be open and honest with everyone, and share your wins and your blessings, as well as your struggles. We can't help you unless you let us know what you need. We can all help each other!

Also, you will find a FREE gift at the end of some chapters. These are action items for you to do on your journey toward creating your 100X Life. Please take the time to participate in them. This is how you will maximize your use of this book.

If there is anything else I can do to help you on this journey, please let me know. I'm looking forward to adding as much value to your new journey as I possibly can, helping you achieve everything God wants for you in your abundant life!

With sincere gratitude,

Stephen Skinner

P.S. Although I wrote this book, I am just like you. We need each other! If you'd like to share life-changing benefits of *The 100X Life* with your friends, family, & colleagues, please invite them to visit *the100Xlife.com*. The more people in the community, the better we can all help each other!

Contents

Preface

God has profoundly opened my eyes to something since the original writing of this book in 2015:

The 100X Life is the pursuit of your best life that God created you to live. I believe the first and last commandments of God to you and me (Genesis 1:28, Matthew 28:19) are one and the same. And that is the blessing to "Be Fruitful and Multiply."

Of course, we had a time in the Garden of Eden where this was true, and we were perfect. This original state of man is known by the ancient Hebrew word *shalom*. Most of us have heard this word, and we immediately think of peace. But similar to the way the word *love* has more than one meaning in Greek, *shalom* means more than *peace* in Hebrew. It means "universal flourishing, wholeness, completeness, and delight."

But we screwed up having this state of shalom. As a result, God told us life will be tough (Genesis 3:17–19).

Fortunately, God sent His son Jesus to not only restore our opportunity at that life by His sacrifice, but to also show us what living in shalom looked like, and to offer it to us. He called it the abundant life (John 10:10).

And before Jesus left this earth, He gave us the same commandment in a different way, but the same commandment. He commanded us to spread *His* fruit, *His* kingdom with everyone we come in contact with (Matthew 28:19).

The enemy who lied and tricked us has been trying to thwart our attempts at fulfilling these commandments from our Good Father. He was successful in the Garden of Eden, and He now works at attacking us from any angle he can, including our health and vitality.

Although I believe The 100x Life will help you move closer and closer, day by day, to this abundant state of shalom, The 100X Life is *not* a promise of prosperity. In fact, it may be just the opposite for you. What The 100X Life does do is give you the strength to face the challenges the enemy and life throw at you without allowing them to take you out.

I stated that in here in 2015, but I had no idea I would be tested to see if I really would practice what I preach.

It came at the cost of a failed business investment from a bad partnership and a financial loss of almost a half a million dollars. And it could have even been worse, but God granted me some mercy from the worst-case scenario we faced from fully materializing.

It was a huge blow to my confidence. I will tell you this: I kept showing up and pushing Play. Every. Stinking. Morning.

I honestly do not know how I would have handled this crisis if I did not have this system. The pressure of life may have just taken me out as it almost did over a decade ago, and as I saw it take out too many other great businessmen and women who frequented my pharmacy and are now nothing like the person I used to know because they chose to numb the pain with too many prescription medications.

I vividly remember one day when I got some pretty disturbing news in the form of a certified letter from an attorney. I immediately went to my office, shut my door, and prayed to my God, who said, "Nothing is impossible" and praised Him by playing "Through The Eye of The Storm" by Ryan Stevenson.

God got me through that day. And the next morning, what did I do?
I pushed Play.

Because as one of my heroes, Rocky Balboa, once said, "It ain't about how hard you're hit. It's about how hard you can get hit and keep moving forward, how much you can take and keep moving forward. That's how winning is done."

I believe God wants you and me to win. It is my prayer that this system He gave me that you will discover in this book does just that for you!

Here's to your pursuit of Shalom!

Stephen

What is the 100X Life?

*"Still other seed fell on fertile soil. The seed grew and produced a crop that was a **hundred times** as much as had been planted!"* Luke 8:8 (NLT).

"You will never change your life until you change something you do daily. The secret of your success is found in your daily routine."— John C. Maxwell.

"If you are breathing, you are still alive. If you are alive, then you are still here, physically, on this planet. If you are still here, then you have not completed what you were put on earth to do. If you have not completed what you were put on earth to do . . . that means your very purpose has not yet been fulfilled. If your purpose has not yet been fulfilled, then the most important part of your life has not yet been lived." —Andy Andrews, *The Noticer: Sometimes, all a person needs is a little perspective.*

Where did The 100X Life come from? The 100X Life is a life of vision and excellence. The system I am going to teach you has come from my daily routine of spending the first hour of my mornings with my advisor, my coach, my best friend: Jesus Christ. It's from listening to and reading God's Word and talking to him. I am no longer alone. One morning in 2014, the verse that led to this book just jumped out at me. I had personally already gone through this transformation, and I was sitting alone with God, thinking, "What can I do to tell others, to help others who are struggling with maybe their health, stress, or business?"

There it was! **Luke 8:8**. It was Jesus talking about these different soils. In that verse, he says, "Still other seed fell on fertile soil. This seed grew and produced a crop that was **100 times** as much as had been planted" (NLT). Later on, his disciples asked him what he meant by that. He basically said, "If your soil is good, if you're working on yourself by spending time with me *first*, if you'll spend time with me, follow me, and work at this every day, you may actually produce 100 times what you are planting!" It's not going to be easy. Like a farmer, it takes daily work at this, but the fruit, oh, man! The fruit is gonna be so good!

I thought, *"Man, that is what I want to do! I want to have 100 times the impact on this world!"* I'm not saying that it's 100 times more money. I'm not saying it's 100 times as much this or that. What I'm saying is, after all is said and done, the only thing we leave behind is how we impact others. That's the vision. That's looking ahead at the end of the road, at the end of our life. We're saying, "Okay, what did God use me to do, to make a difference in this world?"

Let's set our goal at 100 times. We may not get to 100 times impact. We may get to, as he also said, 50 times. Maybe just 10 times, maybe it's just double, and maybe it's just one. What is so cool is that in the same book (Luke), Jesus says that if there's *just one person* out there who turns toward him, a party is thrown in Heaven! If I can just make a difference in one person out there, then I'm going to be happy!

The excellence part comes from another verse that means a lot to me. It's Colossians 3:23. It says, "Whatever you do, work at it with all your heart. Work at it with excellence as though you're working for the Lord and not for human masters." Yes, we have to please people. We need to serve people, but if we'll look to doing things with such excellence like Christ is in the room with us in our day-to-day life, in our business, in leading our families and our careers, we will do excellent work and live an excellent life—one worthy of 100X impact!

We can take these two mindsets with us every day, asking God and ourselves daily these two questions:

1) What can I do to have 100 times impact?
2) How can I live with excellence?

That's the goal. That's what this system will help you with. You will learn tips and strategies to make that kind of impact on others. Then they take it and make that same impact. We build a community around it, and before we know it, we have changed the world! What do you think?

Does this excite you like it does me? If so, great! Let's get started! What are some ways you're going about actually creating a life of 100 times impact in your own personal life?

First and foremost, you need a daily routine you can stick to. John Maxwell said, "If you don't set your agenda every day, the world will set it for you." We will walk through this. It will be simple and practical, and you can do it in your own personal way. You already have most of the tools you need in order to go about the daily system found in this book.

I want to make this process as natural as possible, regarding both the spiritual and physical components. Why? It generally works, if you do the right things, and you have a lot fewer side effects. You hear those commercials, don't you? At the end of the commercial, the announcer says, "Oh, and by the way, this will make your liver fall out, and make this and that happen to you." I know far too well the things that can happen.

I do believe a natural lifestyle and natural medicine are by far the best way to prevent and support chronic medical conditions. That is what I will show you in the book. This is not theory, but practical recommendations that are proven to work. At the same time, I believe in the integrative approach to health and living, meaning if I walk out to my car this afternoon and I get hit by a truck and shatter my leg, I am probably not going to be able to get a herb that's going to take care of that, but too much reliance on mainstream medicine isn't good. I just know way too much information about prescription drugs and doctor visits to recommend mainstream medicine as a first option.

This system is not for everyone, and chances are, if you have been living like I was before I started this process, you are on a prescription med or two, and you have medical conditions. Please always ask your doctor before trying any of my recommendations. You may have a genetic disease that you cannot help, but most of them we cause ourselves by our lifestyles.

It is more important than ever that we take charge of our health, as a growing number of our medical doctors and health care workers (myself included) have left the badly broken healthcare system. Do you really want your health in the hands of government?

How do I know this will work? Because these are things that I've done in my life that has really transformed me and given me a different outlook on how to live. I have shared bits and pieces with others and have seen their lives changed. But I've never shared the whole system until now.

My goal is to give you some forward-thinking ideas to help you grow and find your purpose, live with excellence, and find some fresh ways to live in such a way that you can have that 100 times impact. If you're not feeling well, if you're not taking care of yourself, then you can't have that impact on others; you can't multiply your impact on the world.

If you're reading this and you feel stuck, overwhelmed, stressed, or unhealthy, this book is for you. You just don't feel great about yourself or what you're doing. Maybe what you've been doing hasn't been working. We often hear that the definition of insanity is doing the same thing over and over and expecting different results. If you've been out there and you've been doing the same thing over and over and nothing is sticking, nothing is working, or if you are battling addictions, you are not alone. There are things that you can't fight by yourself. If you ever feel alone, or if you just want to grow and make a bigger difference, keep reading, because those are the things I hope to share in this book. I hope you join the community which will be built around this as well. We need each other, we really do.

So many people want to change their lives, but many never do. We get stuck, frustrated, and overwhelmed with life. We sometimes wake up at 2:00 am and think, "How did I get into this mess?"

Until now.

What if I told you that by reading this book you can learn and implement a natural and even supernatural process that will renew and transform your life?

It will take you from a place of frustration, stress, and misery to a place of happiness, peace, and abundance. Along with that, you will gain more clarity, more energy, and more enthusiasm for life. You may even lose some weight, feel great, and look better, too.

I believe anyone at all can benefit from applying the process outlined in this book: business owners and entrepreneurs, busy mothers, (who we all know are the true CEOs of their homes), pastors, ministry leaders—indeed anyone in leadership.

Have you ever wondered what was in God's mind when he created you? What perfection and plan did he create you for? He saw you and he saw all you could be through the power of his supernatural grace. Are you living up to that potential?

You weren't meant to be overweight, tired, stressed, or overwhelmed. That's not the life experience that God created you for.

In this book, I offer two main goals for you:

> **1.** To look at your life in a different way. I want you to look at your life and intention every day with eternity in mind.
>
> **2.** To implement a set of seven new daily habits. I have seen tremendous benefit from doing so in my own life, and so have others who have followed this method.

We just have a short time here on earth to make a difference. We have a race to run. There's a lot counting on you and we need you. The people around you need you. You're no good to somebody if you're sick all the time, if you're not your best you. You can't be used for all that God wants to use you for if you're overwhelmed if you're stressed if you're preoccupied, or dealing with poor health, a rotten attitude, and a despairing state of mind.

This book can help change all of that for you. You're going to get incredible results in your life. Your focus, your energy, your mental clarity, and your way of dealing with other people will all improve. Most importantly, the fruits of this are the very best offered anyone at any time. Consider this list, found in the Bible, and called the Fruit of the Holy Spirit: love, joy, peace, patience, kindness, goodness, faithfulness, gentleness, and self-control. I have found a way to experience all these in my life, and that's where I want you to live as well!

This book will outline the process that I learned and now use. I will provide my website address and point you to my blog and other online resources for further reading and further exploration. If you will decide that this is for you, and if you will commit to doing this, you *will* succeed.

Author Introduction

As we begin, please allow me first to tell you who I am, so you can better understand why I am so excited about this discovery.

Have you ever planted some really nice flowers that looked great at the nursery, but after about a week they were dying? That was me.

I am, by background, a pharmacist. Well, I am actually an entrepreneur trapped in a pharmacist's body. I have had a 20year career as a compounding pharmacist, a pharmacy owner, and a health food store owner.

Although I did not start with a passion for natural medicine and the old-fashioned art of compounding, over the years it really grew. Like the Jimmy Buffett song about a pirate, I felt like a pharmacist 100 years too late! Pharmacy has been very good to me, and I have felt blessed to have discovered these niches of the profession.

I have started, run, and successfully sold several businesses through the years, some of them in health care. I am now running two companies. One is a real-estate-development company. The other is a business- and life-coaching company, which involves speaking engagements and training, of which this book is a part.

The problem was that I had a lot of success right from the get-go in my career. I really thought it was all me. I thought that it came from my hard work. Indeed, some of it did. But what I was ignoring was the fact that I was given some gifts to be able to do the hard work, to pursue those ventures, and I was being blessed. Instead, I attributed my success only to *me*. I really thought that I was "Mr. Midas." Everything I was going to touch would turn to gold. And, in many cases, it did.

However, like King Midas of the fairy tale legend, this success came at great cost. I really ignored some things in my life. I ignored my children and my wife. I was working six days a week. I was working all the time, often eating all three meals at the pharmacy. I would leave before my kids woke up and return after they were asleep. I even missed a birthday party.

I took advantage of a lot of people, both my employees and my colleagues. I also ignored my health. I was eating whatever I could (often a hamburger), whenever I could, as fast as I could. I was stressed out at work and at home. I was working all the time, just grabbing things to eat really quickly. I was not sleeping well, so I was drinking Diet Cokes in order to get the energy to get through the hectic day. I was finding that my teeth were hurting, and I was grinding them at night.

Then all of a sudden, a few years before I wrote this book, everything just caved in on me. Overnight, my pharmacy lost a major client. With that client went over a quarter of my profits. I was overweight. I had gotten some worrisome reports back from my doctor. My cholesterol was high and my blood sugar was erratic. I was only in my early thirties, but I was overweight, and increasingly bad-tempered.

I started losing people around me. I started losing staff members. I just thought that people were disposable and they were there to serve me. Somebody might have looked at me and thought I had it all, that I was very successful. On the outside I was, but on the inside I was miserable.

I finally came to the realization that all of this was happening because God was reaching out to me. He was telling me, "Stephen, you think you did all this, but you didn't do *any* of this. I gave these things to you and if you don't change some of your ways, I may just take it all away." It became a very lonely, very dark time in my life.

I really didn't know what to do. I had reached a point where I was going to start drinking heavily or do something even worse. At the same time, my father was starting to experience a lot of health problems, including rheumatoid arthritis, arteriosclerosis, and colon cancer, all within a few months. The image of him on the table with tubes going everywhere stuck with me. I remembered how much I despised hospitals. Although hospitals and those who work in them do an invaluable service, hospitals give me the creeps, and they are depressing to me.

I am extremely thankful my wife stuck with me. I put her through some difficulty because of the way I was living. I must frankly state that she is an incredible woman, the most selfless person I know. I tell people *she* is the reason we are still married, approaching 20 years at the time of this writing. It's not because of me!

But even with her patience, I was still in a terrible state. The anxieties over money, work, and my father's failing health, compounded by my neglect of my wife and our children—all of this was destroying me from the inside. The physical abuse I gave myself—bad diet, no exercise, long hours of nothing *but* work— these were destroying me from the outside. I was losing myself and everything that meant anything at all.

That's when the transformation slowly began. God finds any way He can to help us, and my turnaround started in a very quiet way.

We had a dog, and his name was Jake. He was a little mutt and he always wanted to go for a walk. I started taking him out on a walk in the mornings. I started walking. I didn't really know what else to do. It was the only time I had for myself. I was so stressed out throughout my day. I was *still* working 12-hour days and eating all my meals at work, and each day I would come home to a very active house with a young daughter and twins! So I started getting up early and walking Jake while listening to an iPod.

I started searching for anything positive I could find to listen to. I listened to positive music. I started to listen to different podcasts, like Joel Osteen's, John Maxwell's, and anything else I could find that was something positive. I didn't want to hear anything negative.

And even from this bare beginning, changes began to take place. I began to notice the incredible beauty of the sunrise, and how it was different each day. Over time, that morning walk became an oasis of refreshment for me.

Eventually, my dog passed away, but the seeds of change had been sown. I eventually moved from walking to intense exercise, really devoting the first couple of hours of my mornings to my spirit and body. People who knew me started to ask, "What's changed about you? You're looking better; you aren't as negative as you were."

Now I'm in the best shape of my life. My health is great. I sleep well. I have peace. I've got tons of joy that I just want to share with other people. I'm now living with intention. I have a purpose. I tell people I'm now fueled by *supernatural* and *natural power*. I've discovered that *this is the best way to live*.

That's where I am right now, and that is what I want for you. This is my mission in life. I have no doubt in my mind that I would be on three or four different medications, and possibly would have been in rehab by now had I not made these changes!

Chapter 1—The 100X Life Discovery

*"A farmer went out to sow his seed. As he was scattering the seed, some fell along the path; it was trampled on, and the birds ate it up. Some fell on rocky ground, and when it came up, the plants withered because they had no moisture. Other seed fell among thorns, which grew up with it and choked the plants. Still other seed fell on good soil. It came up and yielded a crop, a **hundred times more** than was sown"* Luke 8:5–8.

"You are no good to God, family, your company, or anyone/anything else if you are run down or you get sick or drop dead of a heart attack!"—Darren Hardy

Want to know a really amazing statistic? Read this:

Our death rate is **100%**.

Yes, unless we are some of the few still living when our Lord and Savior Jesus returns, our death rate is, and will remain, 100%. We're not going to stay here forever. We're going to pass on. This life is going to be short.

The question this brings up is, "What are we doing with our short, limited life here on earth? Without something to bring this into our awareness, this question does not spring to mind very often, or we all would probably live and act very differently than we do.

For years, I worked all the time, thinking that was the way to be. I neglected my family, not because I disliked my wife and children, but because I thought I was doing the right thing by working really hard to build a business "for the future" and "to take care of my family's security." There were many other things I thought as well.

They all gave me the same sense of direction, which was, of course, "Keep going! Work even harder!" And, when things began to get really difficult, do you think the running narrative in my head changed at all? No! Not for a long time. Things had to get really bad before I began to realize that my mighty effort wasn't panning out so well after all.

When that happened, I really didn't know what to do. Many of us get into this trap. Usually, the things we come up with as remedies for the problem don't work very well. We get ourselves sick from the intense drive, fueled only by our ambition and sheer determination, but when we're sick, we try to treat only symptoms. This opens the door to further harm.

For instance, we might even be diagnosed with some condition that requires us to take prescription medications. But not only do prescription medications cause side effects, they also cause many nutrients to be depleted from our bodies. Combine this with the fact that most of us are already not eating very well, though we often tell ourselves otherwise. When we add a medication that starts depleting these nutrients even further, it starts what I call a vicious drug cycle.

You think, "Oh, well, I'm just getting older," or "Oh, this is from this condition." It's not necessarily. A medication may be depleting something and there could be a simple natural alternative to replenish that vital nutrient. It's like a car having gas, but no oil. Not going to work too well, is it?

We are made up of spirit, body, and mind. They all need care and feeding.

I'll say it again because it's worth repeating, the definition of insanity is doing the same thing over and over and expecting different results. If you've been doing the same thing over and over and nothing is sticking, nothing is working, and even if you are battling addictions, you are not alone. There are some things you can't fight yourself. With God's help and this easy-to-follow system, you can have the 100X life.

Chapter 1 Bonus

Take a look at where you are now by taking this Personal Assessment. (*http://www.the100xlife.com/soiltest*)

Chapter 2—PLANT

"Great things are not done by impulse, but by a series of small things brought together."—Vincent van Gogh

The Rule of Five

"Picture a tree in your backyard that needs to be cut down. If you grab an ax and take five good swings at the tree each day, eventually you will chop it down. It may take a month to fell a small tree, while a big tree may take years to topple. The size of the tree isn't the issue; the real question is whether or not you diligently take five swings at it every day.

For leaders, a primary challenge is to identify the five activities most essential to success, and then to practice them daily. The Rule of Five doesn't ask: 'What are the five things I would like to do.' That's a question related to passion. Nor does it ask: 'What are five things I should like to do?' That sort of inquiry uncovers your values. Rather, the Rule of Five asks: 'What are the five things I must like to do in order to be successful?' Posing this question cuts to the heart of the daily behaviors necessary to win in your chosen profession."—John Maxwell

Okay, you are still here; that's good news! How was the test? Now, it's time to get to work, time to PLANT! In order to do that well, we must begin with our soil. We have to get our ground prepared so it can produce FRUIT. This is about having a 100X impact on the world. What does that look like?

Darren Hardy wrote a book called *Living Your Best Year Ever* and I have this quote from it taped to my mirror: "True achievement and life fulfillment happens when you have success at home, in the marketplace, and with the triad of your being: your mind, your body, and your spirit."

Good soil is going to produce the greatest harvest, with any kind of crop. Can we agree that with all other things being equal, good soil is going to produce the most?

In Galatians 5:22–23, Paul said, "The Fruit of the Spirit is love, joy, peace, patience, kindness, goodness, faithfulness, gentleness, and self-control. Against those things, there is no law."

If Jesus Christ is your Lord and Savior, then you're living under the influence of the Holy Spirit in this model. You will see these things just naturally come out. They are going to be the product of having good soil. Who doesn't want more love in their life? Who doesn't want more joy, more peace? We're all stressed out, and having things like kindness, goodness, and self-control is huge.

Now, how do we get there? We really can't just snap our fingers and produce these. We all are naturally gifted for maybe one or two of these, but it's not something that we can just produce at will.

These are things that we have to work at every day. Like farmers, we're talking about soil; we're talking about a harvest and the fruit. I am sure you know some farmers, or maybe you even grew up on a farm.

Where I am from (rural Alabama), just about everywhere you drive, you're going to see a farm. If you talk to any farmer, especially dairy farmers, they'll tell you that in farming, you don't get a day off. The cows always need milking. They don't understand when it's the weekend or a holiday.

Not only that but also, farmers typically go through a routine very early in the morning. This is a key foundational practice of The 100X System, and it is critical to getting our soil prepared so we can produce this kind of fruit.

It starts with working on ourselves every single day, just like farmers work every single day. I got this idea and practice from John Maxwell, as you see in the quote at the beginning of this chapter. He has written many books, and when asked how he has written so many, he said he has a system he calls his daily Rule of Five.

There are five things that he does every day, without fail. That's how he's able to produce so many books, so much great content. Have you heard of his system?

This discovery has been phenomenal in helping me grow as a person and to develop my system of seven habits. Now I am introducing my system, which I believe will transform you, and I ask you to trust the system and follow along, but you may (and I encourage you to) develop your own.

I use an acronym to help me remember mine. This acronym is PLANT. This actually becomes a lifestyle, just like a farmer. It's like John Maxwell says, *every day* I'm going to do these things. Does that mean that I'm going to do these on the weekend? Yes! Maybe not to the full extent, but yes, I'm going to do these on the weekend. Am I going to do these on a holiday? Yes! I'm going to do these on a holiday, and so are you!

Here are the seven habits in a Rule of Five format. Every day I'm going to:

1) Pray and Praise my Father in Heaven, my dad. That's the *P* for the plant. I do it as soon as I wake up in the morning. I'm like the farmers. I want to get up early and do these things first. Before my feet hit the floor, I just say, "God, I'm thankful. You've given me another day. I'm going to use this to the best of my ability. I want you to lead me and guide me and show me what you want me to do today, and I'm going to follow you." That's the first thing I'll do before I even get out of bed, every morning.

I am also going to praise him. I am going to thank him for caring for and loving me. This is my Creator! This is my fortune teller! He knows everything about me! He knows my future! He's my coach and he's also my best friend! If we know that there is someone out there who knows our future, knows what's best for us, I think it's a good idea to talk to him and thank him, so the first thing I'm going to do is pray and praise. I'm also going to try to do that throughout the day as much as I can—just little short things before a meeting or before I'm going to speak to someone, or while on a walk, or before or after exercise; after a good meeting, a kiss from my girls, a beautiful sunrise or sunset. It's all worthy of praise!

2) Next is the letter *L*, for Learn and Listen. I'm going to spend time listening to and learning from God first, before reading or listening to anything else. I'm going to spend time in his Word and listening to him and what he wants me to accomplish that day. Then I'll listen to others, maybe to John Maxwell or Darren Hardy through their writing, through their life. I'll listen to words of wisdom from authors, mentors, friends, and family. Podcasts and audiobooks can be great sources as well.

3) Number three is *A* for Act! I'm going to take action and be active. I'm going to act on God's promptings. Maybe I get a prompting from him to text someone a special verse or an encouragement. I'm also going to be active, which for me means exercise. We all need to find something to get our blood flowing every day. We're all at different levels, but if you have a pair of shoes, you can move, and if you have a smart phone or another device, you can listen to good things while you move.

4) Number four is *N*, which stands for Nourish. I'm going to nourish my soul, my mind, and my body every day. The soul part is covered in step 1 & 2, but I just want to emphasize how important it is. We are in a spiritual war! Never forget that! I'm going to nourish my mind through some positive videos, songs, podcasts, and books. As far as nourishing my body, I'm going to do my best to eat cleanly and healthfully. We will cover not only what you put in your body, but what you put on it.

5) Finally, *T* is for Thankfulness. Every day I'm going to be thankful. I'm going to express gratitude—first, to my Father for all

these blessings that I've been given, then to others. I go through a gratitude practice every morning, and I'll share that with you. There's always something that we can find to be thankful for, even if it's not been such a great day.

That is the system of seven habits. You'll notice that each item is a verb, something to do. If we do these things every day, what is that result going to look like? Just like a crop a farmer plants, slowly the good FRUIT will start to come out. Even if you don't do them well every day, if you do these things every day, FRUIT will grow. You're not always going to get all of these five things done every day. There will be some days that you'll forget or something will happen, but try to be intentional about this.

We will cover the FRUIT in more detail in Part 2. Right now, we just need to commit to the system and, as a farmer, trust that the FRUIT will grow.

Because this is not easy to do alone, at the end of this book, I plan to offer a 100X Life Group transformation study, where we're going to work on these things together. This book is the result of my personal transformation. This is my daily routine, and what I encourage you to do, after the study, is to eventually make your own. I am doing this to get you to start. PLANT and FRUIT. We can all remember that, right? Although there are a few fundamental practices, it will become a dynamic system, because you'll go through different seasons in your life. I hope we can build a community of "Dirt Workers" or "PLANTers."

Now the big question as we begin. Perhaps you are thinking, "Stephen, do you actually do all of the seven habits first thing in the morning, or does it just need to happen by the time you go to bed at night? When do you actually do each of these segments?

I do most of them first thing in the morning, and there are a few you *must* do first thing in the morning, but you will find a download at the end of this chapter, and as long as you get them done, go for it! I do realize we are all different, and some have more time for themselves at night. The important thing for some of these is to do them with your Daddy, your Father in Heaven. He wants some one-on-one time with you, and he is going to bring amazing peace, joy, love, comfort, and even challenges to your life that you've never imagined! His Masterpiece will start to be revealed in you.

Why do people really want to use this system? What kind of results can they expect? Is it going to be easy, right away, for you to do, or is it going to take a little while?

It takes a while. It is a slow process; so is farming. That is why I am talking about 100 days of transformation. But, like unto a plant, you will shortly begin to see stems, then buds. How long change takes may be different for each of us because we are all struggling with different things.

As you try to figure out how to do this Rule of Five, there will be challenges. You are going to have struggles. In fact, I am willing to bet you may have more struggles. How do I know this? It has been that way for most people who have done this. You are starting a process of growing closer to God, becoming all he created you to be. The Enemy hates this. He wants you to have no impact at all. Keep this in mind as you go through the journey. I also want you to realize that you can reach out to me and eventually to our community.

Chapter 2 Bonus

Now that you have an overview, we have created a one-page checklist that encompasses the entire system. This is a beautiful color PDF you can print off and hang next to you as you build your 100x Life, or you can use the Editable PDF to check off each day, or use the image as a screen saver to be a constant reminder. It reinforces the 7 Daily Habits you are about to learn in the book. Get yours at *The100Xlife.com/PLANT*.

THE
100X LIFE
DAILY PLANTING CHECKLIST

Now that you have an overview, we have created a one-page checklist that encompasses the entire system. This is a beautiful color PDF you can print off and hang next to you as you build your 100x Life or you can use the Editable PDF to check off each day, or the image as a screen saver as a constant reminder. It reinforces the 7 Daily Habits you are about to learn in the book.

TODAY I WILL:

- [ ] Get up early
- [ ] Say Good Morning to God before anyone else
- [ ] Write 3 Blessings in my Gratitude Journal
- [ ] Spend time with God
- [ ] Offer up Thanks & Praise to Him
- [ ] Journal
- [ ] Pray constantly with Thanksgiving (before any meeting, discussion, or activity)
- [ ] Take my B- vitamins (Bible, Book, or a Blog)
- [ ] Listen to a book or a podcast
- [ ] Listen to an encouraging song
- [ ] Make my to do list: List my Big 3 for the day
- [ ] Exercise (Bonus if I sweat!)
- [ ] Make a smoothie or raw juice
- [ ] Eat 75% Clean or Healthy (Paleo or Mediterranean) or take the best option I have.
- [ ] Smile & Laugh
- [ ] Avoid something toxic: (Media, Foods, Harmful Substances)
- [ ] Speak my affirmations from God or my key #VOD
- [ ] Share my #VOD
- [ ] Add value to someone

Now let's learn about when to PLANT.

Chapter 3—When to PLANT

"As a door turns on its hinges, so a sluggard turns on his bed"
Proverbs 26:14.

"I found evidence that the most productive people in history were disciplined enough to wake up before everyone else did. These people weren't just a little more productive than everyone else; they were more productive by leaps and bounds. George Washington Carver was one of them."—Andy Andrews

This is the number-one thing that's transformed my life: my morning routine. I believe it will transform yours as well.

If you do this, you're going to start sharing the habits of greats like John Lee Dumas of Entrepreneur on Fire, Andy Andrews, John Maxwell, Mother Teresa, Howard Schultz of Starbucks, Tim Cook of Apple, and even George Washington Carver, who was an amazing inventor.

Let's read the scripture, and I believe you'll see where I'm going with this. This is from Mark, Chapter 1 verses 35 through 38 from the New International Version . It says, "Very early in the morning, while it was still dark, Jesus got up, left the house, and went off to a solitary place, where he prayed. Simon and his companions went to look for him, and when they found him, they exclaimed, 'Everyone is looking for you!' Jesus replied, 'Let us go somewhere else, to the nearby villages, so I can preach there also. That is why I have come.'"

Jesus is our model, our example in this. It says he got started very early in the morning while it was still dark. Our goal is to produce 100 times as much as is sown in us. We may not achieve that, but let's do our best.

We do that by making our spiritual soil good. That parable is about having good soil. If you have good soil, then the good fruit is going to come out, which I often mention is Galatians 5:22 and 23, the Fruit of the Spirit. Let me ask you a question: Do farmers who prepare a soil get up late to do that, or do they get up early? Jesus got up very early in the morning.

The other thing you'll notice is he went off by himself to a solitary place, where he prayed. Then, people came looking for him, and when they found him, he didn't respond the way they expected. They said, "We've been looking for you." They're all freaking out, and he doesn't even really respond to their question about being lost. He has a new direction, a new focus. He replies, "Hey, it's time to go on. It's time to go to some nearby villages. I'm ready to go and preach and spread my word there; that's why I've come." He gets up by himself, goes alone, meets with his Father, and now, he has his focus for the day, a new direction! This is why it's so important for us to start early in the morning.

Martin Luther said that he spent the first hour of the day with the Lord unless it was a busy day. When he knew it was going to be a busy or challenging day, then he spent two hours with the Lord.

John Maxwell said that he wakes up often at 3:00 am, and between 3:00 and 7:00 am, he sits in a chair that he calls his thinking chair. That's where he does his best thinking and writing. He has written many books. In fact, he even wrote a book on thinking.

After the day starts, when the world wakes up, you barely have time to think. I know. When I was in the pharmacy, the doors were open at 8:30, and often before that, because people were standing there. From 8:00 am to sometimes 8:00 pm, it was on. A phone call after phone call. "Stephen, this line's for you. Stephen, this line's for you. Stephen, this line's for you. Someone here wants to see you. This person wants to meet with you, and this other person needs an answer. This one wants to ask you about buying an ad for this." It was nonstop all day long. Believe me; I know what I'm talking about when I say the world comes at you later on in the day.

This morning routine is part of taking care of yourself. You have to take care of yourself first before you can effectively lead and take care of others. What good are you if your health is terrible, if you feel terrible, if you're tense, if you're angry? I've been there. I've awakened angry at the world and didn't know exactly why.

What I believe strongly is that we are made up of spirit, mind, and body. We're whole beings, and we have to work on all three of those every day to take care of ourselves. I have a podcast episode where I go into detail about my morning routine as well as an option to get some videos I shot a while ago, showing how I do it. You can find it at *stephenfskinner.com/030*. I go into more detail about exactly what I do, but here I'll say that my goal is three hours.

Three hours from the time I have to leave the house is when I'm usually going to wake up. During the school year when I get the kids off to school at about 7:30 in the morning, that means I'm up at 4:30. Sometimes later in the summer, I push it back to 5:00 or 5:30, but it's always that early because I have to spend the first hour working on my spirit, having time with God, and getting my mind and my focus right. The second hour, I work on my body through exercise, making a post-workout smoothie that has a lot of nutrients, and taking my vitamins. The third hour I spend getting ready for the day, getting my to-do list in order, shooting off some emails, and helping the kids get their vitamins and head off to school.

George Washington Carver was asked by Congress to come and appear before the assembly. He was so fascinating to them that they kept extending his floor time. They asked him, "How do you manage so many breakthroughs? How have you done so many things?" I don't know if you know this, but he developed over 150 recipes for the peanut, and over 100 different commercial uses of the peanut alone.

He said, "Every day, I get up in the morning, even before the birds are awake. I go outside in the trees, and I ask God for my marching orders for the day. I ask God, 'God, what can we create today from this peanut that will help your people?'" Isn't that awesome? Look how the Lord blessed him with all those ideas, all those inventions. It's really amazing.

Throughout this book, I'll give you plenty of resources to go sign up for. Here, I'm just trying to reinforce to you the importance of a daily morning routine. I'm going to challenge you. If what you've been doing hasn't been working, there's time to change it up.

Yes, you may have to set the alarm an hour or two earlier. You may be tired. But you know what, I bet at the end of the day right now you're tired anyway. If you'll just start slowly spending your first hour with the Lord, you'll see the peace and the wisdom that he'll give you.

Start doing some exercise and you'll find that your energy levels will go up. Then you'll sleep better at night. Those hours that you do sleep can be better. I used to really struggle with sleep, and I found that intense exercise helps me sleep so much better. I can't stress this enough.

I want you to do this. It will transform your life.

Okay, set that alarm. Get up early in the morning. Go make it happen!

You now know you need to PLANT, and that you need to do it early in the morning. Let's move on to how to do it. It's time to get to work, time to PLANT! In this book, PLANT is an acronym, and each letter in the word has a specific meaning.

In brief, the components of PLANT are:

Prayer and Praise
Listen and Learn
Action
Nourish
Thankfulness / Thanksgiving

In order to plant a crop, a farmer must first prepare the soil. In our lives, it is the same way. In order to PLANT well, we must begin with *our* soil. We can use the example of the farmer and his work to see what we must do with ourselves.

One characteristic of farmers is that they live very organized lives. Their day revolves around the needs of the farm at all times. Typically, a farmer begins his work very early in the morning, usually before the sun has even risen. This idea of starting the day very early is appropriate to us as well. And how do we start the day? With Prayer and Praise.

Chapter 4—Prayer and Praise

"Rejoice always, pray continually, give thanks in all circumstances; for this is God's will for you in Christ Jesus" 1 Thessalonians 5:16–18.

"Now Abraham arose early in the morning and went to the place where he had stood before the LORD" Genesis 19:27 (NAS).

"But I will sing of your strength, in the morning I will sing of your love; for you are my fortress, my refuge in times of trouble" Psalm 59:16.

"In the morning, LORD, you hear my voice; in the morning I lay my requests before you and wait expectantly" Psalm 5:3.

"Very early in the morning, while it was still dark, Jesus got up, left the house, and went off to a solitary place where he prayed" Mark 1:35.

Prayer

First, we commit to waking up early. You may already be making excuses about that, which is normal, because as soon as we begin to change our lives, we are going to catch some resistance. That's to be expected. Feeling resistance is a sign that this new direction is the right one. After all, it's effortless to sleep in or to stay up late, but the moment we begin to get our lives in order, especially in alignment with God and his will for us, watch out! The good news is, to start this part you only need to get up about five minutes earlier.

We're starting with prayer. Why is it important to pray every day?

I will give four reasons:

- Jesus is our model for leadership. He's the ultimate leader and what did he do? Well, Scripture tells us in Mark chapter 1 verse 35, "Very early in the morning while it was still dark Jesus got up, left the house, and went to a solitary place, where he prayed."
- It's an incredible gift that's been made possible by the grace of Christ. Many people never had the privilege to pray like we can now. Do you realize that in prayer, we can approach the Throne of the Creator? This was not something that was made available to people before Christ's Incarnation. They couldn't just approach the Throne of God. Christ made that available to us. In Hebrews 4 verses 15 and 16, it says, "This high priest of ours understands our weaknesses, for he faced all of the same testings we do, yet he did not sin, so let us come boldly to the Throne of our gracious God. There we will receive his mercy and we will find grace to help us when we need it most." It is an incredible gift that we can do this.
- In prayer to God, we find that we have someone *who understands us*. Sometimes no one understands us, not even our spouse, but yet he does. He understands because he lived on this earth and he went through the same things that we go through.
- Prayer opens up the incredible gift of truth, which is communicated to us by the Counselor (the Holy Spirit). In the second book of Corinthians chapter 13 verse 14 of The Message, we read, "The amazing grace of the master Jesus Christ, the extravagant love of God, the intimate friendship of the Holy Spirit be with all of you."

Now that we know some reasons why it's beneficial to pray, here are three things that we need to do in our daily life: pray first, pray continually, and praise.

Pray First

Pray first, beginning every day in prayer. It brings close the almighty God, Jesus, your friend who loves you; and the Counselor—the Holy Spirit.

As soon as my alarm clock goes off in the morning, I drop to my knees and I pray first before I do anything else. Although we do best to pray in our own words, it is good to know how to pray. For example, our prayer might be something like this:

"Father, thank you for granting me the night's sleep. I ask that you be with me today. Direct my path. I trust in your path and I ask you to help me add value to other people. Help me to bring glory to you. Use the gifts that you've given me to bring glory to you and help others. I place my trust in you. Help me serve you today. In Jesus' name. Amen."

Pray Continually

Now, during the day, we pray continually, as 1 Thessalonians 5:17 says to do. The venerable old King James English rendered this as "pray without ceasing." This is something really remarkable and it seems unrealistic when we are starting out. But consider the following: Have you ever thought about the way you talk to your friends and family? Do you tell your friends, "I shall be back within a moment's time and for now, goodbye." If you're with them all day, do you do that? Or when you're with your family and you leave the room, do you tell them and give them a formal goodbye? Of course not! When we are with our family and friends, there is a constant flow of communication.

In prayer, we speak to our Heavenly Father the same way. Have you ever thought about opening your day in prayer the way I just described, and *not ending it*? Praying constantly is simply keeping a constant dialogue with God all day long. *It is no different than the flow of communication we have with the most beloved people in our lives.*

This constant flow of prayer continues through the day. At the end of the day, we close it out before we sleep. Our prayer might be like this, if it was not such a great day:

"Lord, thank you for being with me today. It was a tough day. I didn't do everything I should have done and I'm sorry about that. Please forgive me."

Or maybe it was a great day, and you pray, "Father, that was an awesome day! Thanks for blessing us with these opportunities, with what we got to experience today."

Then, whichever way your day went, you could say in closing, "I love you, Father. I can't wait to meet with you again, to continue to go through this life with you."

Now, many people feel a bit awkward about prayer. For some of us, it's like going from zero to sixty in nothing flat, and that may feel weird. It is okay if you're not used to doing this. It is also very likely that you will forget to keep it going during the day or will forget a morning prayer or an evening one. Using short prayers, like the ones written above, may help.

As in any earthly conversation, we usually know very little of what we will say until the conversation begins. These prayers help us begin the conversation. After some time, it will grow and deepen into the fulfillment of the command, "pray constantly," and we will understand both what that means and how well it works.

If you have a child, you pick them up at school and you ask them, "How was your day today?"

What do they say? "Okay."

You say, "What did you learn?"

"I don't know." You're trying to find out exactly what happened and what they learned, but your child doesn't open up to you.

There are times when we're riding in the car or we're outside or just hanging out and they'll suddenly start talking. You know what that's like. Well, it's the same thing with our Heavenly Father. Even though we probably have some idea of what happened at school and what our children are going through if we know them well, we still want to hear from them. We still want them to open up their hearts to us and share their thoughts and feelings with us. God is the same way. He knows us. He wants us to be talking with him. He wants a relationship with us. It will get easier as you practice.

Psalm 139 says, "Lord, you're with me, you're in front of me, you're beside me," and he is. When you get that, when you have that constant dialogue, you'll never feel alone. I can be on an airplane, in a hotel room, or anywhere else, and never really feel alone. That's the comfort that having a relationship with Jesus can bring.

Prayer is a conversation with God, but it is also a formative art. We may not be used to the idea that there are masters of prayer, but the fact is that through history there have been many of them. Jesus' own disciples knew that he was a master of prayer, and it is recorded in the Gospels that they asked him, "Lord, teach us how to pray." Jesus' response was the prayer we call the Lord's Prayer. It consists of several very specific elements:

- Glorifying God, a.k.a. Praise
- Thanksgiving
- Confession (acknowledging the things we did wrong, or not so well)
- Supplication

These words carry a lot of potential religiosities, but let's keep this very simple.

Praise
Praise doesn't mean saying meaningless words to God about how great he is. He's great whether we say so or not. But if we have had some sort of experience where he did something for us, we can

connect with him by acknowledging it. If we start our prayer with this, we will find that more and more things for which we can praise God are revealed to us. We simply need to stay honest about what we are aware of.

Thanksgiving is very closely related to praise. Isn't it so with our loved ones here? If my wife gives me a great gift, I say to her, "Thank you! You're the greatest wife EVER!" So, there is a real connection between praise and thanksgiving.

Confession is one word that is horribly misunderstood in our times. Oftentimes we have a big problem with "confession" as if it is something completely awful and looming over us. "God's punishment is coming and you'd better confess!" is a statement many of us are rather crippled by. Happily, such a concept is actually false. The truth is much simpler.

The truth is that we are usually actually punished by our own mistakes. And this usually happens immediately. Any of us who has ever snapped in anger and yelled at someone knows this is true. We feel terrible afterward! We have to go and apologize. That is confession! When we see that we did something wrong, we know we need to go and amend it. That is precisely what happens in prayer. It is not a recitation of dry transgressions against a code of conduct that is forced upon us. It is a very real, honest assessment of where we screwed up. We already know it, and when we tell God and someone close to us about it, things get better. The Lord wants us to be in that joyful mode of praise and thanksgiving, but to do that, we often have to unblock our way by admitting the things we did wrong. That's all there is to it!

Supplication is a sixty-four-dollar word that simply means "Ask." If you look at the sample prayers above, you will see that the things we might ask for are simple: help to see and do the Lord's will throughout the day, to do what is helpful to others, and so on.

There is one axiom that shows up in our prayer examples that is worth mentioning. We do not ask for ourselves to have stuff. "Lord, please give me a yacht!" does not show in the prayer, nor does,

"Lord, please send me a billion dollars!" or anything else like that. Instead, we see, "Lord, help me use the gifts you have given me to help others, and to bring glory to your name." So, there is an element of self-LESS-ness that must be in our prayers.

The truth is that when we live like this prayer says, we are tremendously rewarded. I wrote earlier about my success in business, but also about the simultaneous crash in my health, the impending loss of my family life, and even the crumbling of my business. When it's all about me, eventually things crack. When things are aligned to be about serving the Lord and others, then what is truly important is made very, very good. This has always been true, ever since people began praying to God.

Prayer, praise, and thankfulness are intermingled, as we have seen. If we do not know what in ourselves to praise God for, we can look around us and find plenty. For example, "Hey, thank you: that was a gorgeous sunrise this morning. The weather was beautiful yesterday. Thank you. Thanks for a good night's sleep."

First Thessalonians 5:18 says the same: "Give thanks in all circumstances." And again, in Philippians, chapter 4, Paul said, "Rejoice in the Lord always. Again I will say rejoice, let your reasonableness be known to everyone; the Lord is at hand. Do not be anxious about anything, but in everything, by prayer and supplication with thanksgiving, let your request be known to God."

So, we start with giving thanks before we start asking for the things we want. Sometimes we are really wanting something, but it is best to start with thanksgiving first. Sometimes this immediately helps us put things in perspective. For example:

"Lord, thank you. Thank you for your blessings. I have a car. Thank you that I have a job, a business. Now, Lord, I thank you for that, but I'm having some trouble in my business. Will you help me with this?"

Praise is a very beneficial way in which to pray. In all circumstances thank him.

Why praise? Why praise every day? If you're like me, you have been going through some storms. Believe it or not, it is praising God that helps us heal. We were created to praise.

I remember when the devastating tornadoes came through our town on April 27, 2011, which really wreaked havoc in my state of Alabama. The weekend after they hit, Casting Crowns came to our town and did a concert. They sang the song "Praise You in This Storm." It brought great healing to so many people who had lost their homes or businesses during the storms.

It's the same way with us. We're either in a storm, about to go into a storm, or just emerging from a storm. It is especially that way if we're in leadership positions, whether leading a family or leading a business. Storms come and go.

But we have praise. Praise in worship also helps with depression. I'm not minimizing depression's painfulness at all, but the fact is that when we take our eyes off ourselves and put them on God, depression is sometimes removed from us.

When we realize how amazing God's grace is for us, we can't help but praise. Psalm 130:3–4 (CEV) says, "If you kept the record of our sins, no one could last this long, but you forgive us and so we will worship you."

Don't we feel unworthy, guilty, or ashamed of ourselves at times? Does this sometimes turn to despair? That's not from God. That's from the Enemy. We have to praise our God through this to get out of it. This, like prayer, may feel weird at first, but if we practice, it will start to happen more automatically and feel more natural.

Many people confronted with this thought say, "I go to church on Sunday. Isn't that enough?" The answer, simply, is no, it's not enough. Our lives are meant to be lived in a state of constant praise. This may sound very odd, but it is true. We were made to worship.

First Corinthians 10:31 says, "Whatever you do, do it all for the glory of God." First Peter 2:9 says, "But you are a chosen people, a royal priesthood, a holy nation, God's special possession, that you may declare the praises of him who called you out of darkness into his wonderful light."

How do we praise God? What does this mean, exactly?

There are many ways to understand and offer praise, and they are very simple. We can look at some concrete examples from Scripture that can help us get some ideas of how this works.

Humble Worship

In the Old Testament book of Daniel, we can see this story: "When Daniel learned that the document had been signed, he went to his house. An upper room in his house had windows that opened in the direction of Jerusalem. Three times a day he got down on his knees and prayed to his God. He had always praised God this way."

Daniel's prayer was private, quiet, and very personal. Daniel had a practice of keeping his appointment with God steadily, constantly, under all circumstances. Now, although we do not have the texts of the prayers he said at these times, we do have texts of other prayers he said. In them, we see all the components of prayer—praise, thankfulness, confession, and supplication. It is not reasonable to think that Daniel's own prayer life was without these elements. Indeed, it takes all of these present to pray so much. Daniel's constant, steady, quiet communication with God was both praises in itself, and the place where a great deal of praise to God was expressed.

Think about this passage: 1 Corinthians 15:57 says, "Thanks be to God who gives us the victory through our Lord Jesus Christ."

Commentary about this verse in UNDEFEATED: The Athlete's Bible by the Fellowship of Christian Athletes says, "We serve a God who has never lost. His string of victories is unmatched. He has dominated the competitor with a game plan that cannot be stopped. God is holy. God is mighty. He is undefeated!"

Daniel knew this to be true. This is one of the things that kept him going, even while he was with his countrymen as captives in a foreign land. He knew that the final and enduring victories always belong to God. And he lived it in all his life's circumstances, including the very unpleasant ones, like being in exile, as he was at that time.

If that doesn't get you pumped up, I don't know what will. So there are stories and passages in Scripture that talk about what praise is, what it looks like, and how we can acquire it through considering things "in God's view," which is much broader than our own.

Different Styles of Worship
There are some communities which have a style of worship that can be very energizing and can help us understand some other ways of praising God. One style I'll call "fan style" worship. Similar to what happens in stadiums, it often has a concert of uplifting music accompanied by a sermon that is inspiring.

Some churches have very powerful and inspired singing. If you have a chance, I encourage you to go to the Brooklyn Tabernacle, in Brooklyn, New York. For me, hearing that choir roar in praise and worship was like a glimpse of Heaven on earth. It is an electrifying experience, indeed something that I previously imagined could be experienced only in Heaven.

And what drives this experience? For these people, it is living in the knowledge that our Creator gave his life out of love for us. He brought us from a place of no hope and no chance, and he gave us hope, healed us, redeemed us, and restored us. Is he not worthy of that kind of worship? If we are able to begin to see this truth for what it is, it is impossible *not* to be moved to praise.

We have earthly examples of events that can move us to such fervor. I live in Alabama, and football Saturdays are insane here. We go to stadiums packed with 100,000 people. We watch "tunnel videos," which get the crowd pumped up before the team comes running out on the field. When that team comes out, we go nuts. I've experienced some of the most amazing things at college football games. Incredible victories come, sometimes amidst seemingly impossible circumstances, and we celebrate. We storm the fields. We cry. And why do we do that? Because our team accomplished something unbelievable and defeated the "enemy."

Well, when we put our lives into perspective with how God has done everything for us and saves us constantly, is it not true that the Enemy that God has saved us from is more of a danger than an opposing football team is? While another football team might take the victory of points on the gridiron, the Enemy of our souls and lives wants to destroy *us*. And this is something our God will not allow to happen. Time after time, he saves us, sometimes even when we do not want it. This is an amazing fact, and if we face it, it is far worthier of awe and praise than a victory in any football game is.

In the second book of Samuel, we find this story. "David inquired of the Lord, 'Shall I go and attack the Philistines? Will you deliver them into my hands?'"

This is prayer, right?

"The Lord answered him, 'Go, for I will surely deliver the Philistines into your hands.' David inquired of the Lord, and the Lord answered, 'Do not go straight up, but circle around behind them, and attack them in front of the poplar trees.'" David ends up victorious. What did he do? He celebrated!

"Wearing a linen ephod, David was dancing before the Lord with all his might, when he and all Israel were bringing up the ark of the Lord with shouts and the sound of trumpets."

How about that? He was dancing, but there is even more, and in our times, this is *important*.

"As the ark of the Lord was entering the city of David, Michal daughter of Saul watched from a window. When she saw King David leaping and dancing before the Lord, she despised him in her heart."

Michal was David's own wife. And she was really embarrassed *for* him. She thought he was a total fool. But guess what? David didn't let it bother him.

"When David returned home to bless his household, Michal daughter of Saul came out to meet him and said, 'How the king of

Israel has distinguished himself today, going around half naked in full view of the slave girls of his service as any vulgar fellow would.' David said to Michal, 'It was before the Lord, who chose me rather than your father or anyone from his house when he appointed me ruler over the Lord's people of Israel. I will celebrate before the Lord. I will become even more undignified than this, and I will be humiliated in my own eyes, but by these slave girls you spoke of, I will be held in honor.'"

He didn't worry about her! He was going to celebrate before the Lord!

Often the case with us is that we don't do this—at least we do not do this enough, especially as business owners and leaders. We don't celebrate. We don't celebrate with our family. We don't celebrate with our Lord.

These examples show us that there are many ways praise for God can be expressed. One is very humble, being on our knees in reverence, and there are times for that. At other times we might be like a fan: celebrating, singing, and dancing. There are many different ways to praise.

The thing that is true about our examples is that they are constant. The praise offered by Daniel and David was not just a once-in-a-while event. For these men, it was like a constant stream. At times, there would be more dancing. Other times, there might be more time in the upper room. But no matter what, they lived a life of constant worship, prayer, and praise. It was a daily way of life for them.

Romans 12:1 says, "We offer our bodies and minds as a living sacrifice. Therefore, I urge you, brothers and sisters, in view of God's mercy, to offer your bodies as a living sacrifice holy and pleasing to God. This is your true and proper worship" (KJV).

If this is all new to you, and you've really never spent time in prayer, just hang with me through this next chapter, which will go more in depth on authentic prayer. Prayer and praise need to go together, and that is the *P* of PLANT. The time commitment for this component can range from a few minutes to all day. Now let's move to our next habit: *L*, Listen and Learn.

Chapter 5—Listen and Learn

"All Scripture is inspired by God and is useful to teach us what is true and to make us realize what is wrong in our lives. It corrects us when we are wrong and teaches us to do what is right. God uses it to prepare and equip his people to do every good work" 2 Timothy 3:16–17.

"So then faith comes by hearing, and hearing by the Word of God." Romans 10:17 (NKJV).

"Be still, and know that I am God! I will be honored by every nation. I will be honored throughout the world" Psalm 46:10 (NLT).

"O Lord, you have examined my heart
and know everything about me.
You know when I sit down or stand up.
You know my thoughts even when I'm far away.
You see me when I travel
and when I rest at home.
You know everything I do.
You know what I am going to say
even before I say it, Lord.
You go before me and follow me.
You place your hand of blessing on my head.
Such knowledge is too wonderful for me,
too great for me to understand!
...Search me, O God, and know my heart;
test me and know my anxious thoughts." From Psalm 139 (NLT).

The Life-Changing Couch

Probably the most transformative discovery of this system God gave me very early New Year's morning 2012, on a couch in my in-laws' den in Tampa, Florida. It was just after midnight, and everyone had gone to bed except me. I was sitting on their red couch, which I'm convinced is the most comfortable couch on the planet.

That discovery was the *Daily Audio Bible*.

It stemmed from a simple question I asked myself, as I was alone, pondering the new year.

I knew my life would undergo radical change soon, as I had put my pharmacy that I had owned and operated for almost 20 years up for sale.

What would help me deal with these changes the most? I asked myself.

The Bible.

That would probably help.

Yeah! I want to try to read the Bible through this year.

But how?

I'm soooo busy, how can I do this every day?

These were my thoughts as I sat in the dimly lit room just after midnight.

Why not try to listen to it? was a thought that popped in my head. *You love podcasts. Why not see if there's a podcast where someone does that?*

So I simply went to iTunes and typed in *Daily Bible*.

I discovered a podcast called The Daily Audio Bible that had tons of reviews, all five-star.

So I subscribed and I began to listen.

I didn't realize at the time, but I now know who was clearly speaking to me alone, in the wee hours of the New Year 2012 . . .

Jesus himself was there . . . nudging me.

Just like He did a year or two earlier when He used my dog to tell me, *"Let's you and I start taking a walk together, I got some things I wanna tell you . . ."*

You can hear more about that story by watching this video on my YouTube channel. Search *Stephen F Skinner RPh*. Channel. The video is called *When You Don't Know What To Do, Take A Walk*

Over 2,000 mornings later, I haven't stopped. I can count on one hand the days I've missed.

I don't tell you that to brag. I tell you that because it's become a lifeline for me.

These five verses from Psalms 30 describe beautifully what God has done for me through this ministry, birthed from a man named Brian Hardin, who is just a couple hours up the road from me.

> *"I praise you, Lord, because you have saved me and kept my enemies from gloating over me. I cried to you for help, O Lord my God, and you healed me; you kept me from the grave. I was on my way to the depths below, but you restored my life. Sing praise to the Lord, all his faithful people! Remember what the Holy One has done, and give him thanks! His anger lasts only a moment, his goodness for a lifetime. Tears may flow in the night, but joy comes in the morning"* Psalm 30:1–5 (GNT).

You see Prayer, Praise, and Thankfulness—three of the seven Habits of *The 100X Life*, along with the power of a fresh, new morning spent with the Good Father, all wrapped up in these five verses.

Brian is one of my spiritual mentors as you will see in the acknowledgments. He wouldn't know me if we ran into each other in a store, but he's made a tremendous impact on my life.

Brian simply reads the Bible every day, in real time, following the One Year Bible reading plan, which is Old Testament, New Testament, Psalms, and Proverbs every day. He has a terrific voice that holds your attention, and he also places tranquil music or sounds of nature in the background, which you will notice takes your stress level down a notch or two. Many days, he will provide words of wisdom, and he always ends with a prayer. Takes only about 15–30 minutes, the amount of time one could waste on social media, to listen. Show up every morning, and you will have read the Bible through in a year! Can anyone say, "Bucket List"? I can tell you on December 31st, when you hear his final words, you will experience an exhilaration and joy of having read completely this book for all time. And when you look at yourself in the mirror, you will be different. In fact, after just 30 days, you will begin to notice some things change inside you. I challenge you to test me and see!

Not only does Brian read the Bible each day, in real time, fresh every morning, but the *Daily Audio Bible* also has prayers after the reading, that people from all over the world can call in to request.

In my opinion, it is the most beautiful picture of what God intended His church to look like.

In fact, one morning, I heard a young man who called into the prayer line that *rocked my world . . .*

His name was Jake, and he was incredibly distraught.

He said his father had just committed suicide.

He didn't know where to turn, but he called into the DAB Prayer line.

I remember feeling upset for him, praying for him, and then thanking God that of all the places Jake could've turned to, he called his brothers and sisters from around the world.

Jake mobilized a worldwide army of prayer warriors!

You can buy an app from your mobile app store for the Daily Audio Bible for free. I like the app, because it is easier to pause, rewind, and download meaningful episodes if you wish. Also in the app is Daily Audio Psalms and Daily Audio Proverbs, which is a chapter of the book of Psalms, or a chapter of Proverbs, in five minutes or less per day. I encourage you to buy the app, and take some time and listen for yourself. I challenge you to listen to it for 30 days in a row. After the 30 days, if you are not seeing any change or benefits, email me and I'll send you a dollar to pay you back for your investment.

Now, if you are reading this book in any electronic format, do you realize the significance of what you're holding in your hand? Even if you're reading this as a print book, I would guess that your electronic device is within arm's reach right now. That's the case for most people. Almost everything you need to build your 100X life is in your pocket or your bag via your mobile device. You can access the Bible online, using any of a number of sources. As I just mentioned, every morning, I sit down with a nice cup of coffee and I listen to the Daily Audio Bible podcast (*http://dailyaudiobible.com/*) while reading along on a Bible app on my iPad. In Daily Audio Bible, Brian Hardin reads the Bible fresh, in real time, every day. He also uses the sounds of nature in the background, making it peaceful and interesting. He changes the translation each week and makes it easy for even the busiest person to take in scripture every day. I really don't think we modern-day Americans realize how precious a gift the accessibility of the Bible that we have now really is. Allow me to further explain.

Don't Eat the Fish

This might have been the headline of *The Paris Times* in autumn of 1572 if such a newspaper had existed. Why? I read this article entitled *"When Christians Died for the Bible,"* and it made me think about this. August 24th, 1572, is known as St. Bartholomew's Day, and on that day, Frenchmen began slaughtering 100,000 of their Huguenot countrymen throughout France—10,000 in Paris alone. Their favorite disposal sites were the rivers of France, which were stained red by the blood. The rivers of crimson would have made the fish unsafe to eat for months.

It was the bloodiest week in the history of the Huguenots, otherwise known as French Protestants, and it's the blackest day in French history. Their story is marked by unrelenting episodes of harassment, property seizures, tortures, executions, and slaughters.

Calvinistic Christianity, which would eventually triumph in the formation of America, was born from their ideas. Their steadfast faith in the face of death is an everlasting testimony to the Church in all ages.

The Huguenots were different in three ways. First, they were literate at a time when only the clergy and nobility could read. Second, they were economically independent of the old agrarian feudal system of land-owning nobles and land-working serfs. Most were artisans and business owners. Third, they wanted a participatory Christianity, where they could read Scripture themselves and meditate upon it on their own to determine its meaning.

This was a bottom-up system of Christianity and is in great contrast to the medieval Roman Catholic Church with its mass and its priests at the head in a top-down system. The Huguenots hungered for self-expression and freedom in their worship, in their business pursuits, and in their government. For this, they were persecuted in a medieval world that was not ready for the idea.

They were basically Christian entrepreneurs and business owners, which is who I am writing this book for. That would have been us. The rights that we take for granted, from freedom of religion to the right to bear arms, are all influenced by the Huguenot experience. The blood that was shed into the French rivers of 1572, which contaminated the fish and would have resulted in the headline I mentioned above, may well have been the original seed for our American faith and government.

When you read anything, especially the Bible, you hold in your hands something that people literally have paid for with their lives, and it didn't cost you much in comparison. You can download a Bible app straight to your device for free from Youversion (*https://www.youversion.com/*) or Bible Gateway (*https://www.biblegateway.com/*).

The second letter in PLANT, *L*, stands for Listen and Learn, which is what the French Protestants strove for, and we should, too.

We have opened our day with prayer, both praising God and asking for his help. Now, we are going to spend time listening to and learning from God. It is very important to make sure we always do this first, before rushing off into the day. After all, we just spent some time talking to God. Do we then run away before we hear his response? Would we do this in any conversation with an earthly friend? Of course not! So, we stop and listen, and learn what God might have to say to us before going off and reading or listening to anything else.

I learned to spend time reading the Bible and then quietly considering what I have read. Often through doing this, I gain some insight into what the Lord wants me to accomplish that day. Incidentally, one of the great tools we have in our time is the handheld device, such as a smart phone or tablet. On these and many other devices, we can store audiobooks, podcasts, music, and ebooks, including the Bible and many great commentaries on Scripture. So, we can spend this listening and learning time in greater convenience than ever before in history.

"God Told Me Today . . . "

Do you ever hear people say this phrase, "God told me today . . . ?" It is a pretty bold statement, but it is feasible to tune in to what some people call "uncommon sense," that is, seeing our lives the way God does.

Buck Jacobs, the founder of the C12 Group, has coached business owners for over 30 years. He has shared a lot of wisdom in that time, and he states that the number-one thing he would tell anyone to do for true success in business and life is to spend the first hour of their day with the Lord. Why? It doesn't seem to make sense. Well, a great reason is given in Joshua 1:6–9.

> "Be strong and courageous, because you will lead
> these people to inherit the land I swore to their
> ancestors to give them. Be strong and very

courageous. Be careful to obey all the law my servant
Moses gave you; do not turn from it to the right or to
the left, that you may be successful wherever you
go. Keep this Book of the Law always on your lips;
meditate on it day and night, so that you may be
careful to do everything written in it. Then you will
be prosperous and successful. Have I not commanded
you? Be strong and courageous. Do not be afraid; do
not be discouraged, for the Lord your God will be
with you wherever you go."

Who are you leading? Is it your business? Do you have staff,
employees who are depending on you for their family needs? What
about your own family? Your spouse? We're all leading someone,
and indeed, some of us are tasked to lead a lot of people. This
passage shows us how to do that leading: with courage and faith that
the Lord himself is with us, and to meditate on his Word.

Getting into prayer and into reading Scripture are the way we start
the day. Some of you may be asking, "What does this have to do
with the 100X Life?"

Everything!

If you try this for a week or two, I think you'll see what I mean. I
want to challenge you to begin. No matter when you are reading this
book, whether it's the first of the year or late November, you can
start. Just start. As with so many important things, the best time to
begin is. . . NOW!

Remember that Martin Luther was famous for saying that he
spent his first hour with the Lord every day, but if he had a busy day,
he needed to spend two. Another example I'll tell you about is Jesus
himself. Jesus was *very* busy in his short time on earth, especially
during his ministry, but in Mark 1:32–33, we're told, "That evening
when the sun set, people brought him everyone who was sick, and
those possessed by demons. The whole city had gathered at his
door."

Are you busier than he? Do you have a whole city coming to you to solve their problems? How did he handle that? In Mark 1:35, we're given the answer, the example. It says, "Very early in the morning, while it was still dark, Jesus got up, left the house, and went off to a solitary place, where he prayed." I want you to think about who you're meeting with, what this person is, and what he can do for you.

Let me ask you again. If your largest client or your biggest customer wanted to meet with you early in the morning for breakfast, would you do it? Of course, you would. You would get up early for that important meeting. This is no different.

Just think about who you're meeting with, who you're listening to, and what you need as a business owner or a leader. You need an **intercessor** to stand up for you. You need a **mentor** to guide, teach, coach, counsel, and train you. You need a **challenger** to dare you to venture beyond your dreams and an **encourager** to give you strength when you don't feel like going on. You need a **partner** to share in your wins and your losses, and a **confronter** to keep you honest with yourself. Finally, you need a **savior** to give you life more abundantly now and eternally (John 10:10), and spiritual well-being.

That's listening to God's Word, but listening also involves prayer as well. It is how we communicate and have a relationship with God. It's a *two-way* communication. It's not just us talking to him; it's not just us throwing up all over him our needs and our wants, but listening for—and listening to—his responses to us.

Before you start listening to or reading God's Word, ask the Holy Spirit to reveal what he wants you to know. Thank Jesus for allowing this line of communication, for what he did on the Cross that allows us to have access to his Throne. Then open up this Word of Life, this living Word, and listen to what he wants for you. He wants to speak to you, not to a big group of people in a church service, which is great, but he wants to speak to *you*. He wants to meet with *you* every day. He's always going to show up. The question is, will you?

Luke 8:15 says the seed that fell in good soil stands for those with a noble and good heart who hear the Word, *retain it*, and for persevering produce a crop.

How are you going to retain it? Very simple. Get in the habit of writing down what you become aware of during this listening time. When it's on paper, you can look at it later, and what is written may be the thing you need to get through a particularly tough moment. Or, it may be a reminder of something you noticed in the morning but forgot in the sweeping rush of the day.

We hear the voice of God through Scripture from the Holy Spirit through the thoughts—the promptings—that hit us during this time. These promptings can be anything from a feeling of conviction to an idea; it may be a reminder not to talk back to suchandsuch person. Pretty much every day, I'm convicted as I hear about something I need to do better or something I messed up on, and every day I am thankful for something which causes me to praise him. This formula for living works better and better the more we use it.

Learning

Have you ever wondered what transforms a sports team member from an unknown to a starting player? Why did they excel later on in their professional career? Further, why is it that some people start out as stars and then become total flops when they get to the professional level?

My belief is that our motivation changes. Maybe some decide to get really serious about what they do, and they rise to stardom. Others may lose interest, and therefore motivation, and turn into flops.

There is a saying that the world is made up of *C* students. Thomas Stanley, the author of *The Millionaire Next Door* and *The Millionaire Mind*, surveyed a group of people who were quite wealthy, carrying a net worth of at least $10 million each. He wanted to see what they had in common, and he uncovered two facts:

1) They were doing what they loved.

2) Although not everyone attended college, those who did had an average GPA of only 2.7, *not the 4.0 that we emphasize and tend to think about as being of utmost importance.*

When I was in pharmacy school, I didn't make the best grades. Some thought I wouldn't succeed in school or my career, but what happened after graduation was quite amazing. Many of my classmates took jobs with chain pharmacies and received strong guarantees, six figure incomes, and large signing bonuses. I made $36,000 my first year, about a third of what they made. It wasn't until my fifth year of running and owning a pharmacy that my income skyrocketed above the six figures and even up to four or five times what those classmates earned.

Along the way, I was blessed to have won several awards in the practice of pharmacy. I turned out to be a very good pharmacist. In fact, I still have my pharmacy license and still practice from time to time for people. But, oddly enough, never once in my 20 years have I been asked to move a carbon chain like we were taught to do in our organic chemistry classes. Never once has anyone asked me a question about their medication and said, "Wait, before you answer that, what were your grades in pharmacy school?"

Why did I win those awards? Why did I advance beyond my former classmates? Simple. When they began working, they stopped learning. When I began working, I continued learning. In some ways, that's when I really *started* learning. Learning continuously will help you as well.

Here is a sad statistic: One out of every four Americans did not read a single book last year, according to Pew Research as reported in *The Atlantic- The Decline of the American Book Lover.* That number of nonreaders has tripled since 1978. Let me ask you something. If you had a chance to meet and get inside of the head of some of the world's greatest influencers, history makers, and geniuses—to spend time with them—wouldn't you want to do that? That's what reading books can give you, and you can do it at a low cost with programs like Kindle Unlimited, or even at no cost, through your public library.

I believe we should learn something every day. We shouldn't stop learning until the day we die. We are always either growing or dying. We were not created to stay where we are. Paul said this about our faith with the statement in Hebrews 5:11–12: "We have much to say about this, but it is hard to make it clear to you because you no longer try to understand. In fact, though by this time you ought to be teachers, you need someone to teach you the elementary truths of God's Word all over again. You need milk, not solid food!"

It's the same way with our spiritual walk with the Lord, regarding the daily practice of listening and learning. That can apply to our faith, but it can also apply to our professions. It can apply to being a better spouse, a better parent, a better leader. How? Reading! I have come to call what I read "the Vitamin Bs": the Bible, books, and blogs.

Reading the Bible is the great central point in the learning part of the PLANT system. We ought to read the Bible every day. This book has already presented a great deal of information that shows how useful and profitable it is to read the Bible constantly.

There are some books that we might read repeatedly, once every year or so. These include the classics, both of fiction and nonfiction. There are books aplenty about one's desired business or trade techniques. Why did I include fiction here? Because sometimes a great way to be inspired to new ideas or innovations is to get outside the normal view of the world. Books have inspired many people to create all manner of devices and gadgets, which have advanced our level of technology. Life sometimes can imitate art, and through reading, we can find new things to aspire toward.

Blogs are another potential source of learning. Most blogs are people's own personal websites, where they share their thoughts and, in many cases, where you can respond and weigh in on what they have to say. Some people are true thought leaders, and reading their musings is often amazingly helpful. Pick people both in and out of your industry; pick people you want to emulate and learn from.

An alternative means to reading, and ideally, a *complementary means* rather than a replacement is listening. We may listen to audiobooks, but there is also an enormous amount to be learned from podcasts. Podcasts are talks—often given by great authorities in a field—that are recorded and posted on the Internet, very often without charge. Sometimes while listening to a podcast by a master in a given field, we can learn an amazing amount of material that might go right on by us in a book format. When we hear someone's *experience*, it is often the most powerful tool for us to use to improve our own lives. While I am out doing leisure activities, I am also usually listening to something, and often that something is a podcast.

Another widely accessible format is video. There are thousands of video clips on YouTube alone, giving instruction in just about anything imaginable. I have learned how to replace toilets and fix all sorts of things from watching these clips. Some people offer true online courses on YouTube, covering subjects ranging from learning a new language to making musical recording techniques, to buying or selling real estate. I learned enough about real estate to be able to open a venture in the self-storage industry. I first started learning about it through an online course. Then, I went to a conference to amplify my knowledge.

Learning is so important that I would like to make a very specific suggestion. I encourage you to establish a budget for learning, training, or education. As an example, consider this: Try to live off 75% of your income; keep at least 10% to give to God, 10% to save, and 5% to use for learning. This money can be dedicated to continuing your education in your industry, or learning what you need to be able to change fields. There are many different and powerful venues for learning.

Conferences are valuable because not only are you able to set aside some focused time to learn while you are at them, but you are also able to meet people in that particular field. I learned many things about compounding pharmacy from a conference. I learned a lot about natural medicine from conferences, too. We hadn't even thought of this in pharmacy school, but I learned it through reading and attending conferences and seminars.

Through conferences, I've met John Maxwell, the leadership expert. I got to visit his home. I've met Dave Ramsey, the well-known money expert. Anyone can go to those conferences. You can meet these people and learn directly from them. Furthermore, there is a great opportunity in the networking you can do with others who are also involved in the same studies. You can learn so much and develop long-lasting relationships.

Mastermind groups bring like-minded people together. When you do that and you help each other, powerful things can happen. Iron sharpens iron. It truly is a phenomenon. You may be struggling with something that you can't see but others immediately can see, and you will learn a great deal from them. Nothing will advance you further and faster than a mastermind group.

Mentorship is priceless. Go work for someone for free. I think this is a lost art in our country. I worked as an apprentice and learned many things I wouldn't have learned any other way. Early in my pharmacy career, at a conference, I met a man who was far more expert than I was at compounding and natural medicine. I wanted to pick his brains for everything he knew. So I just asked him, "Can I come spend a couple of days working for you? I'll work for free, doing whatever you need me to do; I'll take out the trash—anything. I will do whatever you need me to do, just to see how you do things and learn from your pharmacy." I can't tell you how many thousands of dollars I made from what I learned in those few days.

I did the same thing as I was exploring the idea of opening a self-storage facility in 2014. My wife and I loaded up the car and we headed out. We visited storage facilities in Tennessee, Kentucky, Indiana, and Illinois. We met and learned from other self-storage business people. Why reinvent the wheel? You can learn from so many people out there.

We can learn from our mistakes. A mistake is an opportunity to learn. I have failed at times. It's okay to fail! We can learn from our failures and mistakes. We may be striving for 100%, but we're going to make mistakes. When we do, we just have to think about them, process them, and learn from them.

Learn from others around you. You can learn from your employees. Be a "noticer." I've learned so much from my coworkers over the years. I learned from a young man how to live out my faith. I watched him. I had this impression before that it wasn't fun to be a Christian, but this guy showed me. He displayed such quiet strength, such wisdom, that he intrigued me and I wanted to be like him.

You can learn from the people you work with. A fellow pharmacist always displayed such joy and enthusiasm and love of people. I learned so many healthy living tips from my manager at my health food store.

You can learn from your family and friends. I've learned a lot from my children. I can't even begin to tell you how much I've learned from my wife!

All the knowledge in the world won't change your life if you don't put it into practice, so let's move to the next chapter, *A* for Action.

Chapter 6—Action!

"Then the Lord said to Moses, 'Why are you crying out to me? Tell the people to get moving!'" Exodus 14:15 (NLT).

"Let us think of ways to motivate one another to acts of love and good works" Hebrews☐ 10:24☐ (NLT) ☐.

*"Do not merely listen to the Word, and so deceive yourselves. Do what it says. Anyone who listens to the Word but does not do what it says is like someone who looks at his face in a mirror and, after looking at himself, goes away and immediately forgets what he looks like. But whoever looks intently into the perfect law that gives freedom, and continues in it—not forgetting what they have heard, but **doing it**—they will be blessed in what they do"* James 1:22–25.

"In the same way, faith by itself, if it is not accompanied by action, is dead" James 2:17.

"We all come into this world the same: naked, scared, and ignorant. After that grand entrance, the life we end up with is simply an accumulation of the choices we make."—Darren Hardy, *The Compound Effect*

"There is one thing that 99 percent of 'failures' and 'successful' folks have in common—they all hate doing the same things. The difference is successful people do them anyway. Change is hard. That's why people don't transform their bad habits, and why so many end up unhappy and unhealthy."—Darren Hardy, *The Compound Effect*

"You never know with these things when you're trying something new what can happen. This is all experimental."—Sir Richard Branson

"Make Each Day Your Masterpiece"—John Wooden

"Do NOT say you 'can't'! You can say, 'I don't want to.' You can say, 'I'm not willing to put forth the effort.' But DO NOT say you CAN'T!"
"Don't say 'I can't,' say 'I presently struggle with.'"—Tony Horton

"Just keep pushing play."—Tony Horton

"The graveyard is the richest place on earth, because it is here that you will find all the hopes and dreams that were never fulfilled, the books that were never written, the songs that were never sung, the inventions that were never shared, the cures that were never discovered, all because someone was too afraid to take that first step, keep with the problem, or determine to carry out their dream."—Les Brown

You are most likely reading this book for one reason: You want results. You want something to change. You're tired of the way things have been going. Nothing has changed. You're frustrated. What you've been doing has not been working as well as you'd like, and you want results.

You cannot get a result without an action.

In this chapter, I'm going to show you why you must act and be active and how to do it. You saw the quote above about the richest place on Earth. Bronnie Ware was an Australian nurse who spent several years working in palliative care, caring for patients in the last few weeks of their lives. She recorded their dying statements in a blog called "Inspiration and Chai," which gathered so much attention that she put her observations into a book called *The Top Five Regrets of the Dying*.

Ware writes of the phenomenal clarity of vision that people gain at the end of their lives and how we can learn from their wisdom. When questioned about any regrets they had or anything that they'd do differently, she says, "Common themes surface again and again." The most common regret of all was, "I wish I had the courage to live a life true to myself, not life others expected of me." She discovers that when a person realizes that their life is almost over and they look back clearly on it, it's easy to see how many dreams have gone unfilled. Most of the people had not honored even half their dreams and they had to die knowing that it was due to choices they had made or, worse yet, not made.

Health brings us a freedom that few of us realize until we no longer have it. Live with no regrets.

One thing that can reboot your system is this 100X Life method. The system of PLANTing every day gives you time with God and it may stay with you, like those promptings you'll get as you start to listen to God. I hope you've started doing this every day. I want to ask you, what are you doing with those promptings?

Remember the story of Jesus and how when He got really busy on Earth, he did something that we sometimes don't: he took action. He kept going. We find in that Scripture, from Mark chapter 1, that the whole town came to him, wanting him to heal them. What he did the next morning in verse 35 was to get up early, before sunrise, and go somewhere by himself to pray. What's interesting is after he emerged from that, he was ready with his plan for the day! Not only did he say it, he acted on it!

Mark 1:36–39 in God's Word® Translation reads, "Simon and his friends searched for him. When they found him, they told him, 'Everyone is looking for you.' Jesus said to them, 'Let's go somewhere else, to these small towns that are nearby. I have to spread the good news in them also. This is why I have come.' He went to spread the good news in the synagogues all over Galilee and he forced demons out of people." He was ready to go, and he acted. He didn't even pay attention to their question about where he had been or their comment that everybody had been looking for him. He's like, "Let's go! We've got more work to do! Let's go!"

How many times have you had "Sunday morning resolutions," sitting there in church, moved by the worship or the sermon, intending to make a change? You knew what you needed to do, and you had good intentions. You wanted to change your life. You wanted to use your life or business for good, for helping others. You knew you needed to take better care of yourself so you could be more effective, of more use to God. *You wanted to change*! But then Monday morning arrived, and you didn't change anything.

The Compound Effect is a great book, written by Darren Hardy. In it, he writes this gem, "There is one thing that 99% of failures and successful folks have in common. They all hate doing the same things. The difference is: Successful people do them anyway. Change is hard. That's why people don't transform their bad habits and why so many end up unhappy and unhealthy."

People who succeed and those who fail *all hate doing the same things*. We all hate doing the same things, for the most part. The difference is the successful people do them anyway, all the time.

Some of us indeed roared out of the gate with new changes, but shortly afterward we fizzled out, and in no time were back to business as usual. Why is this?

Some people make a mistake in that they go too hard, too fast. Their mighty effort feels exhilarating at first, but it is not sustainable. Once the feeling of inspiration runs out (and that can happen very quickly), the lifestyle change also winks out of existence.

The process we are learning here is precisely not that amazing rush of changes. Instead, this is about a daily walk, a daily process that we do day in and day out.

Mark 4:20 reads, "But the seed planted in the good earth represents those who hear the Word, embrace it, and **produce** a harvest beyond their *wildest dreams*" (The Message).

What is your wildest dream? Psalm 37:4 says, "Take delight in the Lord and he will give you your heart's desires" (NLT). When you get that desire, when you get that prompting, it is of the Father. It's coming down from Heaven to you. The same Psalm later says this (37:23): "The Lord directs the steps of the godly. He delights in every detail of their lives" (NLT).

He said, "The Lord directs the steps of the godly." He directs a person's steps *but the person has to take them.*

Does this always give us what we want? No. Will we fail? Yes. We will fail. But, we also learn from our failures. However, in truth, these are only opportunities to learn. What will we learn? It depends on the situation. Sometimes we learn a different process of action to get what we want. But sometimes we learn that what we wanted was itself mistaken, and we learn that we ought to desire and pursue something different.

Not trying is more regrettable than actually failing is. Continuing with Psalm 37, in verse 24, we find this: "Though they stumble, they will never fall. The Lord holds them by the hand" (NLT).

Notice what it says there. It says you *will* stumble. Did you know that a plane flies off course 80 to 90% of the time? But, by constantly making little course corrections, it gets to its intended destination.

In the same way, our day may start with a particular goal in mind, but we find that we often have to adjust what we do and how we handle things throughout the day. Many times those changes were not expected, but in the moment, they became necessary. The process we go through in life is the same one a pilot goes through for his aircraft on a flight. As the situation arises, what course correction is necessary? This is the question we face all the time. Usually, the changes are small. Little changes, progressing day after day, will keep us on course and move us to our goal of producing the 100X Life.

How can we know what these corrections are, or what to do? One way is to act on these promptings every morning. The prompting you get could be to pray for someone or it could be to take some other action, or as I like to say, "just push play." Tony Horton, who runs the exercise programs of the P90X brand, says, "Keep pushing play.

Keep pushing play." What he means is just show up. He's not asking for you to be perfect, just to show up.

Luke 8:15 covers the parable this book and my podcast are based on. Luke writes, "But the seed on good soil stands for those with a noble and good heart, who hear the Word, retain it, and by **persevering** produce a crop." Darren Hardy echoed this thought in *The Compound Effect*, where he insists, "Small, smart choices plus consistency plus time equals **radical difference**." He goes on to say "It's not the big things that add up in the end. It's the hundreds, thousands, or millions of little things that separate the ordinary from the extraordinary."

What I've noticed over the last few years of using and teaching this system is that you shouldn't necessarily act immediately on every prompting you get, and it may not be what you think it is. Maybe the thought you have is, "Sell everything and move to India to be a missionary." It may be good to sell something and pray for and support someone in India, rather than go there yourself. When a prompting comes, write down what you think it is, talk to God about it, and then go about your day. You may find that within a few days, you'll run into somebody and they will tell you about an opportunity to support a mission or project that's going on in India, for example. It's amazing how that works.

If there are big promptings—maybe to start a business or to do something radically different with your life—if you get that prompting over and over, and if it's something that just won't leave, start paying attention to it. For instance, I had a prompting about making a podcast. I couldn't let that go. I had this message that I kept being prompted to get out. I had to get this book out. It wouldn't die. It wouldn't stop. My prayer and hope is that it will change more lives than it already has.

My podcast, the 100X Life Show (*http://www.stephenfskinner.com/podcast-2/*), has simply been taking the Scripture readings that I've read during my morning quiet time, as well as my thoughts and what God has told me about that particular passage, and applying them toward running a better business or being a better leader. I had some ideas when I first launched the podcast. I recorded some different episodes. I had different formats I was intending to follow. I did them and they just didn't feel right, but I still felt like I needed to do the show. I kept following God's promptings and I ditched those and just kept on recording.

If you've listened to my podcast episodes, you know they're very authentic. I don't stop and I don't edit. If I sneeze, if I cough, it's on there. One thing I know is that the episodes flow freely. Once I started, once I followed his prompting to do that, he has given me an unbelievable amount of material. At last count, I have over nine hundred episodes in my queue, which I could release at any moment.

People look at me when we talk about acting and doing little things every day, and they say, "You're so lucky." I actually did an episode on this called Lucky or Smart: (*http://www.stephenfskinner.com/episode-2-lucky-or-smart/*). I'm not always so lucky. For instance, one thing I acted on was a health food store I opened a few years before I wrote this book. I had to try it. I had big dreams for it. I wanted to create a small chain of them. It didn't make it, but I knew I had to try. I tried it, it didn't make it, and I'm fine with it. It wasn't meant to be, but I learned a lot from having tried it.

The worst thing you can do is not try, not act. The bottom line is take action.

TAKE ACTION = RESULT.

NO ACTION = NO RESULT.

You can take no action. You can take no action on this book. God gives you that choice. I'm giving you that choice. I feel this book is in your hands for a reason, but God gives you that choice. You can take action or not. Maybe somebody gave this book to you and you've never become a Christian. Maybe now is the time to take action and allow God to save you, allow Jesus to save your soul and the Holy Spirit to give you abundant life now and eternal life forever with God. If that's you, if you're feeling that prompting, then contact me at *www.the100xlife.com/contact*. I would love nothing more than to walk you through that process.

James 4:14 says, "Yet you do not know what your life will be like tomorrow. You're just a vapor that appears for a little while and vanishes away" (NAS). We don't have much time here on Earth. We've got to take action. The wisest man who ever lived, Solomon, wrote in Ecclesiastes 11:6 (CEB), "Scatter your seed in the morning, and in the evening don't be idle because you don't know which will succeed, this one or that, or whether both will be equally good." I love that Scripture because that's telling me, "Throw your seeds out. Go give it a shot. Be diversified." I love diversification in business. If you know me, you know I always have been diversified in my investments and in my business, because, just like this says, you never know what's going to succeed.

He also said in 5:18 of the same book, "Even so, I have noticed one thing, at least, that is good. It is good for people to eat, drink, and enjoy their work under the sun during the *short life* God has given them, and to accept their lot in life."

What are the things that we need to act on? Number one is God's Word, his instruction. Maybe it's something the Bible says to act on—to help orphans and widows, for example, or to help those who are in jail or sick. Maybe it's just to love, to forgive. We don't always like that. Maybe it's a prompting to repent. Don't wait; repent. Maybe it's a prompting to praise. Praise! Praise God! He's done great things for you. He's given us a beautiful planet to live on. Praise him! Maybe it is a prompting to do good, to act on something good that he's just told you.

There's a verse in the Bible that says, "Let us not become weary in doing good" (Gal. 6:9–10). Maybe the good thing we can do is to encourage someone. I'm amazed at how many times I've gotten a prompting to encourage someone and I've sent them a text of the Scripture I read or maybe a link to a song and they all respond, saying, "You don't know how badly I needed that right then." That, my friend, did not come from me. It came from above. God knows how to put all these things together. Maybe it's to be bold and courageous, to not fear man, but to share your faith to let other people know about this good news. Be bold and courageous in what you're trying to do. Maybe it's a deal. Maybe it's a presentation. Do not fear. Act on that.

While we're in this chapter on action, it's time to get up, put your earbuds in, put your shoes on, and get moving. While you're at it, grab a pen and a paper and jot down the actions that come to mind. This is the time to move, to create action. You might keep reading right now, but at some point, I do want you to get up and do that, especially if you're listening to the audiobook of this.

I want to ask you something. I've told you that I'm a pharmacist and that I evolved into being a natural pharmacist and really got into natural medicine. Part of that was because of my own health and transformation, which led to this book. Part of it was from seeing the results my patients experienced on natural medicine.

What if I told you about a pill I formulated that would do all these things?

- increase your HDL
- lower triglycerides
- prevent high blood pressure
- prevent cancer
- prevent strokes
- prevent Type II diabetes
- alleviate mild to moderate depression and aid in severe depression
- prevent insomnia
- increase energy
- increase productivity, and even
- increase libido

As a side effect of that pill, you may lose weight. How much would that cost? Guess what. All of these benefits and more can be found in exercise. Before you roll your eyes and say, "Here we go again," please stay with me as we go to the second part of this chapter on action.

This part of action is made up of two things as we're going through this daily process:
1) Exercise and
2) Your daily to-do list

They go together. Why? Actually, after this quiet time that we start with every day—prayer, listening to God, learning something, and even some praise in there—I move into the to-do list and preparing for action for the day. Why a to-do list? If you don't set your daily agenda, the world will do it for you. That's why it's so critical that you do all of this first thing in the morning before the world wakes up, because by the time the world wakes up, the phone is going off, the texts are coming, and the emails are piling up. You've got to do this before that starts.

Have you ever had a day where all you did was to answer e-mails and texts? By the end of the day, you got home and you thought, "What did I do today? What did I do to move the needle forward today? Nothing." All you did was answer e-mails, texts, and phone calls, and put out fires. That's why you need a to-do list. There are all kinds of apps that you can get for your to-do list. I'm not going to go into that with this book. There are different ones you can use, or you can just do what I've done over the years, which is to use a piece of paper and write it down. I do currently use an app called Trello for my projects and planning, but then I also break them down and write them out on a daily to-do list. You need to do this.

"Let's go! Let's go! Let's go! I'm 45 . . . going on 46! I don't believe in aging . . . Whatever. I've got your aging right here, okay? I believe in moving and eating well. All right, let's jump some rope!

Take care of your body, and it will take care of you, because time keeps ticking and you keep getting older. You can get better or you can get all gooey, crotchety, old, pathetic, icky, gross. Not me, not into it," says Tony Horton in P90X/Kenpo X.

You know what, Tony? I'm not into that, either. I hope you're not as well, Reader. Obviously, I'm a big Tony Horton fan. He makes fitness fun. I have really enjoyed and gotten into the Beach Body products, especially P90X.

The reason why those have been so appealing to me: they help me manage stress. You may remember that I was a completely overwhelmed, frustrated, stressed-out, miserable guy. When I do these exercise programs first thing in the morning, I often think to myself, "This is the worst thing I'm going to face today."

As the current Southeastern Conference Commissioner, Greg Sankey, says about exercise, "Most days, I have a win in my day before most people have their first cup of coffee." Exercise also helps with sleep. Being stressed out is one thing that interferes with restorative sleep. That's from cortisol. Cortisol is a hormone that people's bodies produce when under a great amount of stress. It's involved in the "fight or flight" stress response. People's bodies are created to run from danger. The problem is when we're driving in six lanes of traffic (which were two-lane dirt roads a hundred years ago), then we're getting bombarded by text messages and phone calls, we get to the office, and it's chaos there, and we come home to screaming kids . . . our bodies are not equipped to handle that and they produce excess cortisol.

Cortisol causes your heart rate to rise. It causes you to be unable to sleep, and to be hungrier, which causes you to eat more. Eating more causes you to gain weight, and it can create numerous other health issues. High-intensity exercise will help you sleep much better. It can also help with depression. I've been there. The average entrepreneur can deal with over 100 issues a day. The highs of an entrepreneur can be really high: getting that deal, breaking a sales record. The lows can be really low. They can be very depressing.

What people don't realize is that business owners sink our savings and so much of our heart and soul into our businesses, and when things aren't going well, it can cause depression.

One study done on depression (including severe depression) and walking, showed that not one person reported feeling worse after walking. There's another study that compared exercise to prescription antidepressants. Exercise worked faster and lasted longer. There was less relapse into depression. Plus, my two cents: exercise doesn't make you a zombie like antidepressants do. I've seen that change in many people as I've dispensed antidepressants to them over the years.

There are five common things entrepreneurs face, which are major frustrations: insufficient profit, people problems, lack of growth, hitting a wall, and feeling overwhelmed. Those can cause anxiety and depression. Exercise has been proven to be as effective as drugs for depression. It's also needed for everyday life: being able to do things like chasing your kids, bringing in the groceries, and working in the yard.

All these tasks require functional fitness. There's no better fitness than functional fitness, and in my opinion, there's no one better at functional fitness than the *Beachbody* line of home workouts.

Beachbody is a rapidly growing group of home-based fitness workouts. Many of their workouts include functional fitness, nutrition, and coaching programs designed for this everyday functionality. They incorporate a simple system of body movements, personal coaching, and healthy nutrition that makes you a better athlete. You say, "I'm not an athlete. I'm not a professional athlete." Yes, you are! We all are athletes at some level. Being an athlete makes you a better, fitter, and healthier person. Check them out, go to their website *beachbody.com*. Most of their programs are 60 to 90 days. You follow them and you get a great sense of accomplishment when you complete one! Note: Most of their programs are based on working out six days a week. I average four to six days per week due to life. Some mornings, I meet with a small group; some mornings, I have to take one of my children to school early; some mornings, I just have to rest or do a seven-minute workout. Some of the workouts that I have completed are P90X, P90X2, P90X3, Insanity, T25, and 22-Minute Hard Corps. My personal favorites are P90X3 and 22-Minute Hard Corps because they are shorter (22–30 minutes) and my favorite coach, Tony Horton, is the leader. Tony is funny and motivating to me. He is the modern-day Jack LaLanne, who is known in America as "The Godfather of Fitness." As you can see in this book, I quote Tony often. You spend every morning with him for 90 days, and you will too!

You may be saying, "Okay, that sounds good. You're talking about Beachbody P90X, Insanity, this 'Functional Fitness.' I went to the website. I can't do that stuff." Number one, *you can*. They can scale them for you, with a person who always is "modifying" the workout on a less-intense level. No matter your level, you take a baseline test and work on improving from where you are. Number two, if that's too much for you or if you don't have the money (remember, the 100X Life is a simple system that you can do with not much money), you don't have to start there. In fact, I didn't start there. I started with walking, as I mentioned at the beginning of the book.

If you are blessed to be able to walk, you can exercise. If you can't walk, maybe you can get in a pool and do some water aerobics or swim. How about a bike? How about rowing? I know you're busy. You can't compromise your time with God in the mornings. I've got a batch hack for you, to save you time. To best utilize your time, exercise while listening to Scripture. Get your handheld device and go to the Daily Audio Bible. Get the app or download it from the podcast. Put it on, push play, and start walking.

How about walking out from your location during The Old Testament segment, which is usually 10 to 15 minutes? When you finish the Old Testament segment, turn around and start heading back. During that time, you'll hear the New Testament, Psalms, and Proverbs. Then, you may hear a prayer and some comments. Hey, if it keeps going and you're into it, keep walking. No one said you have to stop right then. Make another lap. Keep walking.

Just 25 minutes of brisk walking a day can lengthen your life by up to seven years. The European Society of Cardiology Congress says that regular exercise could reduce aging and increase the average lifespan. A professor of cardiac diseases and sports cardiology at Saint George University of the NHS Foundation Trust in South London, Dr. Sanjay Sharma, said for the average person in their 50s and 60s, moderate exercise reduces the risk of dying from a heart attack by half. He said, "This study is very relevant. It suggests that when people exercise regularly, they may be able to retard the process of aging. We may never avoid becoming completely old, but we may delay the time we become old. We may live younger when we're 70 and may live into our 90s."

Exercise buys you three to seven additional years of life. It is an antidepressant. It improves cognitive function. There's evidence that it may retard the onset of dementia. You say, "I don't have 30 minutes. I don't have 25 minutes." The Daily Audio Bible averages about 20 minutes a day. If you don't have that, how about a five-minute walk? Daily audio Bible also has a daily audio Bible Psalms or a daily audio Bible Proverbs. Those are five minutes a day. Can you at least do that? If you're struggling with depression, the Psalms are where you want to go. Try Psalms and five minutes of walking. Do it for a month and come back and let me know what's happened. You're going to notice the change.

What about Proverbs? If you have big decisions in your life, such as if you run a big organization, you need wisdom more than anything. Try five minutes in Proverbs every day. I know you can do five minutes. Maybe you don't have much time, you don't want to walk, you don't know what to do, or you don't have expensive equipment or very much room. Maybe you live in a place where it's cold or the weather is not very good. I want you to look for a way to exercise. You can go to YouTube and find so many little, quick five- or seven-minute exercise videos on YouTube. There's one that I do regularly. It's the Dr. Oz's Morning Workout (*https://www.youtube.com/watch?v=RCdrgruVNdg*). It's about seven to nine minutes. It's a great combination of yoga, stretching, and calisthenics. By the time you've done that, you've done about 50 pushups and 20 situps.

Sometimes, if I only have 15 to 20 minutes, I'll bust out the Dr. Oz video. You can watch it on your iPad or your phone. It's free. I'll watch that, and then I'll use the Scientific Seven-Minute Workout (*https://www.youtube.com/watch?v=ECxYJcnvyMw*). High-Intensity Interval Training (HIIT) is doing high-intensity, 30-second exercises. There are 12 exercises you do. One lasts 30 seconds, then you rest for 10 seconds, and then you go to the next one for 30 seconds. It's been shown that these high-intensity workouts are more effective. They are equivalent to doing the longer workouts in a shorter period of time. That's my favorite 15- to 20-minute workout: Dr. Oz's Seven-Minute Workout, followed by the Scientific Seven-Minute Workout.

The Scientific Seven-Minute Workout is by Life Hack. The famous Entrepreneur On Fire, John Lee Dumas, is a big fan of it as well and has created his own variation of it. Doing the Dr. Oz morning workout first provides a great wake-up, a great stretch that gets the blood flowing. Then the higher intensity Scientific Seven-Minute Workout really gets the heart pumping and makes great use of time.

Just start with walking, start with a five- or seven-minute workout. Equipment isn't necessary. Shoes aren't even necessary to do those workouts.

A word on stretching and yoga: If you had told me 10 years ago that I'd be doing yoga, I'd have laughed at you and said you're nuts, but I've actually fallen in love with it. You don't have to follow the Eastern philosophies or religions of yoga. A lot of Christians say that's kind of out there. I'm talking about it from a stretching, balance, strength aspect. You do feel really great afterward. It's amazing. It works on the joints and tendons. You should try it.

There's not as much joint pain involved with yoga as there is with high-impact exercise. Yoga is a great opportunity to humble oneself and pray while doing what Tony Horton calls "working out the kinks." It's a great time to pray, to thank God for the time you have. Your stress will come down so much. Many people avoid exercise because they don't like pain and don't like to sweat, although sweat is a great detox. We'll get into that more in the nourish chapter. Our skin is a large organ and it keeps a lot of toxins. You release a lot of toxins through sweat. It's not a bad idea to have a goal to try to sweat every day during your workout or other activity.

Exercising releases endorphins, which are natural painkillers. You may find that although you may experience a little pain when you begin a program, your day-to-day aches and pains may eventually go away. I'm not saying you should jump right in with something that could be dangerous and therefore needs doctor approval, although it is wise to check with your doctor before you begin any workout. If you're experiencing pain, don't continue. I'm not saying to work out when you're injured, but mild aches and pains, especially after age 40, are very common. There are some things you can push through.

Think about athletes. Why can athletes who get severely injured rehab and come back, but you think you can't? They do it because they know they have a lot riding on their performance. Their whole career is riding on it. Well, so is yours. You need to be as effective as you can. Before you completely blow this off, saying you can't do it, have you ever seen the video of the injured soldier who couldn't even walk but started doing yoga? If you haven't, please watch that video (*https://vimeo.com/41271653*). It is inspiring. If he can do it, you can do it. I'm going to address more pains such as headaches in the next chapter, but you can find exercises for whatever condition you're in. You can do it.

The bottom line is when we take action, it's a win. Don't discount this. This is the secret sauce, the missing ingredient. Taking action and exercising on a daily basis can help a person go from feeling like a "two" on a scale of one to ten to feeling like a "nine" or "ten" after.

When you'd rather feel like a "nine" or "ten," do some exercise. At the end of the day, you win.

Find and do what you like. You may hate swimming, but you may love running long distances. Find what you love to do. It may be hiking, biking, anything you can do outside. Play golf, but walk instead of riding the cart.

There's a man in my town who has been walking all over the golf course (which is pretty hilly) every day for about the last 40 years. He's in his mid 90s but looks like he's in his mid 70s. It's really amazing. Find something you love and get active. Move every day. Play in your day. What's the amount of time you're going to spend on this? Exercise doesn't have to take a long time. It's your choice. Spend a few minutes making your to-do list. Spend a few minutes with your exercise.

Taking your to do list with you when you go exercise may be helpful. Why? I find that I get so many ideas and inspirations while I'm exercising. Maybe you're going to listen to the Bible or something else while you're doing your walking. Record a short note about it on your to-do list, or just make a mental note while you're walking. When you hear a verse you like or want to study more thoroughly, make a note, "That was at the nine minute mark. I want to go back and highlight that verse." The time involved is 15 minutes to an hour—your choice. Cost can be as little as zero. Remember, you can do some of those workout videos in your home for no cost.

By now, I hope and pray you're starting this routine of prayer and praise, a quiet time of listening and learning, and now, action. Action is physical; it involves our body. We're going to continue this thought in the next chapter, Nourish.

Chapter 7—Nourish

"And so, dear brothers and sisters, I plead with you to give your bodies to God because of all he has done for you. Let them be a living and holy sacrifice—the kind he will find acceptable. This is truly the way to worship him. Don't copy the behavior and customs of this world, but let God transform you into a new person by changing the way you think. Then you will learn to know God's will for you, which is good and pleasing and perfect" Romans 12:1–2 (NLT).

"Trouble finding time for YOU? Try scheduling your exercise, meals for proper nutrition, enough sleep, mental relaxation & recreation for recovery. Then go down the rest of your priority list & start adding family, business & social obligations. You are no good to God, family, your company or anything/anyone else if you are run down or you get sick or drop dead of a heart attack!"—Darren Hardy

Part of action in our daily routine of PLANTing is the next letter of PLANT: *N* for nourish. What do I mean by nourish? Plants need fertilizer to produce an abundant crop. So do we, if we're aiming for 100 times the impact.

Nourishing the soul, mind, and body every day is important. The soul part was addressed in the *P* and *L* sections, but I just want to reinforce how important it is. We are at war! Never forget that. Most of the time, the battlefield is between our ears far more than it is outside ourselves. I'm going to nourish my mind through positive videos, songs, podcasts, and books. There are all kinds of positive videos and podcasts that you can listen to. Good music has an incredible ability to fill you with positive energy.

As far as nourishing your body: do your best to eat cleanly and healthfully. It's important to take care with not only what is put in it, but what is put on it. There are a great many things we can do to take care of our body, including taking vitamin and mineral supplements, juicing, and simply resting and relaxing—two things that are easily forgotten about in America.

From Lasagna with Tomato Chunks to Green Juicing and Yoga

Back when my wife and I got married, I was a different person than I am today. I was a very picky eater growing up. My bad attitude, my negative thinking, and my picky and unhealthy eating habits led to an incident my wife has never forgotten. One of the first meals she prepared for us as a young married couple was lasagna. I came home from work stressed out, and I told her I didn't like it because it had tomato chunks.

If you would have told her that the man who refused to eat lasagna just because it had bigger chunks of tomato than he was accustomed to now eats primarily greens, vegetables, and salads, and even does raw fruit and vegetable juicing, she would have said you're nuts. I wasn't taking care of my body by exercising, either. If you would have said that this guy who was pretty much a cereal, chips, Coke, candy bar, and hamburger eating dude who didn't really exercise would now be juicing, and even doing things such as yoga . . . If I can change, anybody can change.

Put the Oxygen Mask on Yourself First

On an airplane, what do the flight attendants tell the passengers before takeoff? They start going through all of the safety procedures and they tell us if we're with a child, to put the oxygen mask on ourselves first before helping anyone else. That's the same way we should look at taking care of ourselves. You have to take time to take care yourself before you can be a good leader and a good provider to others, whether it's your family or your company. This is not selfish. Adopting the mindset that you are taking care of yourself out of love for others may make it easier to do.

Darren Hardy says, "You are no good to God, family, your company, or anything or anyone else if you are run down or you get sick or drop dead of a heart attack." Doing something for yourself is not a selfish act; it's a sustaining act. When we look at juggling all of life's responsibilities, what matters most? You can have a lot of wealth in the world, but if you don't have your health, what good is it going to do? How are you going to enjoy it?

In a university commencement address, Brian Dyson, the current CEO of Coca-Cola Enterprises, spoke of the relation of work to one's other responsibilities. He said, "Imagine life as a game in which you're juggling some five balls in the air. You name them work, family, health, friends, and spirit. You're keeping all of these in the air. You will soon understand that work is a rubber ball. If you drop it, it will bounce back. But the other four balls, family, health, friends, and spirit, are made of glass. If you drop one of these, they will be irrevocably scuffed, marked, nicked, damaged, or even shattered. They will never be the same. You must understand that and strive for balance in your life. Unfortunately, too many find this out the hard way. If you're not carving out time to rest and replenish, to exercise and to monitor your spiritual well-being, then eventually you'll break down. When that happens, you're no good to anyone."

I don't want that to happen to you. It happened to me. I broke down. I don't want that to happen to you, which is the reason this book exists. My belief is that we are not just our bodies. We are spirit, body, and mind. My discovery after all the years practicing pharmacy was natural medicine. I mentioned in the earlier chapters that I was an old-fashioned pharmacist. Like Jimmy Buffett wishing he was a pirate 100 years too late, I was a pharmacist 100 years too late. For some reason, the old-fashioned compounding, and natural medicine just appealed to me.

As I started bringing in more natural medicine, nutritional supplements, and herbal remedies, I noticed that three types of customers emerged in my pharmacy. One group was made up of people who took nothing but medications. I would suggest a supplement to help alleviate the depletion caused by a prescription medication they were on, and they would just look at me and say, "If my doctor didn't say to take it, then I'm not going to take it." These people looked and acted older than their chronological age. Some had victim mindsets. Some had grumpier dispositions. They looked and felt worse than their age indicated they should.

The second type of customer I noticed was what we would call the all-natural customer. These people were vibrant, they were sharp, and they would appear and act younger-looking than the first group. I would see some who were maybe 20 years older than what they appeared to be. I would hear them make statements such as, "You know, I'm in my 70s and my family always said I was crazy for taking all these vitamins and supplements, but none of them have lived past their 50s, and I'm still here." You could just see a difference in them. You could see it in their spirits and their attitudes. They didn't have a victim mindset. They took their health into their own hands. They didn't listen to the traditional mainstream media and medical communities, which are so biased toward the large pharmaceutical companies and the medical industry. They ignored that and they took responsibility for their own health. They learned as we talked about the in the last chapter. They learned on their own. They took control of their health.

Then the third category, which I would say contains most people, is the hybrid patient or customer. That was the person who may just now be getting exposed to the natural options and doesn't really know what to do. There are so many choices out there. He may be on a cholesterol medication or a blood pressure medication that he really doesn't want to be on, but he doesn't really know what else to do. He would be willing to try something natural if it was something he knew he could trust to be safe and effective.

The problem with natural medicine in the United States is that it's not regulated. There's no consistent enforcement of standards. There are a lot of opportunities for being scammed. You have to go with someone who is knowledgeable, who knows the right dose for you.

That's another problem that people experience with natural medicine: they don't take the right product, the right quality, or the right dose.

Someone suggests to them the benefits of fish oil, for example. They go to the large big-box store and they buy the cheapest one they can find. That typically is not going to work. Then they go back to their doctor and say, "You know, it didn't work," and their doctor says, "See, I told you so." It's all due to the fact that they chose the wrong product, the wrong ingredients, or they took maybe one per day when they really should have been taking four to six per day. That's the other thing you have to realize with natural medicine: It's a slower process and it takes more effort, more work, and quite often more doses.

The discovery of natural medicine led me to use nutritional supplements, which are part of the transformation that this book's about. It eventually led me to open up a health food store that I named Living Well Natural Store. Our mission of Living Well was to change lives and empower others to live well by utilizing our God-given natural resources.

What I believed to be true wellness was represented in the store's logo. It has two leaves sprouting out to both sides, and a circle in the middle. Each part represents an aspect of complete wellness. One leaf represents the mind. Another represents the body. The circle in the middle represents the spirit. We cannot achieve total wellness unless we work on all of them. That's how God created us. Also, the spirit is at the top because we are spiritual beings with a body, not the opposite. It all starts with the spirit.

~ 84 ~

The plant also represents healing that can be found from nature. God gave us plants to feed and to heal us. Genesis 9:3 says, "Every moving thing that lives shall be food for you. And as I gave you the green plants, I give you everything" (ESV). Ezekiel 47:12 conveys, "And on the banks on both sides of the river there will grow all kinds of trees for food. Their leaves will not wither nor their fruit fail, but they will bear fresh fruit every month because the water for them flows from the sanctuary. Their fruit will be for food and their leaves for healing" (ESV). Genesis 1:12 says, "The earth brought forth vegetation, plants yielding seed according to their own kinds, and trees bearing fruit with their seed, each according to its kind, and God saw that it was good" (ESV). Psalm 104:14 praises God's provision: "You cause the grass to grow for the livestock and the plants for man to cultivate, that he may bring forth food from the earth" (ESV).

Praising and reminding people of God's provision of these natural things is the purpose of the logo. Also, the plant represented the olive tree. The circle not only represented the spirit, but it also represented the coconut. The olive tree and the coconut are two incredible plants that can be used for food as well as for healing. The health benefits of both are really quite remarkable. Only an almighty Creator can make plants that can do so much good for man.

We've covered the spirit already. It is the first and most important way to transformation. The spirit was part of the *P*: pray, prayer, and praise; the *L*: listening to God and learning; and then in the most recent chapter, the *A*: action and acting on the promptings of his Word and the Holy Spirit. It is the first and most important way to life transformation, as the Scripture so adequately describes it in Romans 12:1 and 2. It is the way out of any type of addiction or stronghold. I firmly believe that anything that has control over us—whether it's alcohol, prescription drugs, or even food and diet sodas—is a spiritual warfare battle as well as an indication that the body is craving something. Until we're willing to go there and fight at that level—the spiritual level—our efforts just won't last in this transformation. We can't do this on our own.

Why is that? As I stated earlier, it's because we are spiritual beings with a temporary body, not a physical body with a temporary spirit. Our world tries to fool us with all these ads for clothes, weight loss programs, etc. But the more we can strengthen our spirit through the process of becoming more like Jesus and allowing the Holy Spirit to be strengthened in us, the more we can have self-control (which, by the way, is Fruit of the Spirit) and the self-discipline to take care of ourselves.

While I'm on the subject of addiction, I want to point out something very important, and I want to challenge you. In this process, you have to remove or at least decrease some things in your life. However, you can't just take everything away. It won't work. You have to replace something that you're addicted to with something else, something that's beneficial to you. Someone may have an addiction that is due to an obsessive-compulsive nature. Perhaps they need to replace that with exercise, such as training for a marathon or triathlon. A negative addiction has to be replaced with something else. Otherwise, there is a void, and that will just lead to problems.

You don't have to become a professional athlete, but you can still learn from them. A couple of summers ago, we had the fortune of getting to visit One Buc Place in Tampa, Florida, where my wife's family is from. It was absolutely mind-blowing to see the emphasis that a professional sports team puts on taking care of their investments, their athletes. The nutritional staff, the massage therapists, the sports psychologists, the physical therapists, and the trainers really have it down to a science at the professional level, and even at the collegiate level now.

Why? Because the athletes are valuable investments to the team owners. So are you. You must start looking at yourself the same way these athletic franchises are looking at their athletes. They know they have to keep their athletes at their best physically, mentally, and nutritionally for them to perform at a high level. That's what you are called to do as well. Remember Colossians 3:23? "Work willingly at whatever you do, as though you were working for the Lord rather than people" (NLT). He demands your excellence. You should give that to him. Your family and all the people who are working for you and with you are all depending on you, and you have to be excellent.

In this chapter, we're going to address the body and the mind, which is our thinking. We've already covered nourishing the spirit, but we're going to talk about nourishing the body and nourishing the mind. We'll start with nourishing the body.

Nourish the Body

There are two ways we can nourish our body. Number one is to eliminate toxins and number two is to replace them with good, clean nourishment. Toxins are all around us. They're in our environment from cigarette smoke, vehicles all around us, and insecticides and herbicides, which are so prevalent everywhere. They're even in our tap water. Our tap water contains what are called halides, chemicals which are put in there to keep the water sanitary. Yes, we do need that for sanitary water, and we don't need to take that for granted. But these chemicals can wreak havoc on our bodies, on our thyroid, on our brain. They can even lead to cancers.

Fluoride is dangerous. My family has been fluoride-free for about ten years now. Once I discovered the harmful effects of fluoride on our brains and bodies, I made the decision for our family that we would not use fluoride. There are a lot of good options out there for maintaining healthy teeth, including fluoride-free toothpaste. Since we've switched, we have not seen any cavities. It's a myth that teeth need fluoride. If you take care of your teeth from a hygiene standpoint, you don't need the fluoride.

Other toxins include many vaccines. Mercury is in a lot of vaccines, among other preservatives that just aren't meant to be in humans.

Our family's been flu-shot-free since 2010. We haven't had a case of the flu. We use things such as elderberry extract, olive leaf extract, vitamin D, and even an essential oil called Thieves Oil to keep the flu from our family. Does that mean we're never going to get the flu? No, but when it comes to those who get the flu shot and those who don't, in my experience, people who get the flu shot catch the flu much more often than the people who don't get the flu shot do. The shot's not 100% foolproof, and it has risks.

Foods also contain toxins. I could do a whole chapter on just one kind: artificial sweeteners. But I'm not going to for the sake of the focus and brevity of this book. Just know that all artificial sweeteners are bad, whether aspartame, acesulfame potassium, or saccharine. Our bodies are not meant to have those. I believe that a lot of people are walking around with migraine headaches, fibromyalgia, ADD and ADHD in children as well as adults—all kinds of conditions—as a result of these artificial sweeteners. We know now that when it comes to an insulin response, the human body responds the same, if not more strongly, to these artificial sweeteners as it does to sugar. It's not doing you any good to use artificial sweeteners. I recommend, if anything, to use stevia, which is a natural sweetener. But you also have to use it sparingly. Overdoing something like stevia isn't healthy.

Reduce sugar. Too much sugar is also a toxin to our bodies. Start thinking about going to unsweetened tea over sweetened tea. Start with doing half and half if that's all you can do. Your taste buds will eventually adjust and you can do this.

I hear all the time, "I just don't like water." I'm not suggesting that you drink tap water. Many municipalities have terrible-tasting tap water, and it all has added chemicals. There are sources of purified, great-tasting water. If you don't like the taste of water, add things such as lemons to it. Make your own natural lemonade without all that added sugar. If you have to add a fourth of a cup of lemonade and the rest water, that's still a lot better than all lemonade. Start with half and half. Then try to go to three-fourths to one-fourth of unsweetened tea to sweetened tea. Those are some little tricks that you can use.

Sodas have no place in our diets. They contain phosphoric acid, and to get that out of the body, the body must attach a molecule of calcium to every molecule of phosphorus. Sodas literally suck the calcium out of the body. No wonder our teeth and bones are weak.

Let me ask you a question while we're talking about sugar. Which is worse, the Budweiser truck or the Little Debbie truck? A few years ago, I was driving down the road after our town had a controversial ruling of finally going wet, which means that it became legal for people to buy alcohol in our town. One day not long after the law was changed, I was driving down to our grocery store and saw a Budweiser truck and a Little Debbie truck parked beside each other. I thought to myself, *You know, which one's worse?*

There is no denying that alcohol can wreak havoc on a lot of people's lives. It can be habit-forming, and it does alter the mind. But I'll also tell you that sugar is every bit as habit-forming and addicting as alcohol or any other drug. In the documentary *Hungry for Change*, which I highly recommend, Jamie Oliver says, "Sugar, when taken in excessive amounts, can lead to cravings and addictions quite similar to those with alcohol and tobacco. Yet we have no problem labeling them as drugs." As Jason Vale says in that film, "It is illegal to give a child cigarettes and alcohol, and so should it be, but it's not illegal to give them white refined sugar or refined fats."

He also says, "We're allowing ourselves and our children to become addicted to this substance, causing soaring rates of obesity, one of the leading causes of preventable death." He goes on to offer ways to kick the cravings for good.

What are some other things that we need to eliminate which are toxins? There have been numerous reports of the exploding obesity epidemic since high fructose corn syrup came onto the scene. It's in so many things. Sugar is often disguised, but just know that anything ending in "-ose" is a sugar and is something that you should try to limit or avoid.

The next item that is on the toxins list is shiny produce. What do I mean by "shiny produce?" Shiny produce is the produce that is not organic, basically. It's been sprayed with plastic wax coatings and pesticides. You should eat organic whenever possible. Some produce, such as apples and blueberries, contain high levels of pesticides. Coffee is another example. I love coffee but coffee is very pesticide-laden, so it's important to get organic coffee. Always try to go for the non-shiny produce, the organic items, whenever possible.

Also, eliminate any type of GMO crops. Pretty much all corn and all soy need to be removed from your diet. When actors have to play a role that they need to fatten up for, they'll eat a lot of corn. We get too much soy already in our diet. Excessive amounts of soy can interfere with the thyroid and hormone processes in the body.

Consider reducing or eliminating most grains, breads, wheat products, and potatoes and chips—especially anything white and refined. Gluten is a toxin to so many people. *Wheat Belly* is a highly recommended book which covers the concerns about wheat and other sources of gluten.

Next is dairy. If you must use dairy, go organic. Try things such as almond milk and coconut milk, which are excellent alternatives that taste very good. Also, the same goes with creamers. There are some other good options out there. If you look at your traditional flavored creamers, there are many words on there that you can't pronounce. It's not good.

Next is MSG (monosodium glutamate) or flavor enhancers and artificial colors or dyes. There are certain additives that always contain MSG. These are what Dr. Russell Blaylock calls excitotoxins. They cause neurons in our brains to fire when they don't need to be firing and are linked to many problems, including migraine headaches and ADD/ADHD in children and adults. These chemicals are disguised under many names as well.

Change Your Oil

Going from margarine and trans fats to olive oil, coconut oil, and butter from grass-fed cows can cause a dramatic improvement in your health. There's something that came onto the scene in 2014 that I'm a fan of: Bulletproof Coffee. Making a Bulletproof Coffee involves using grass-fed butter and coconut oil, or MCT oil (which is similar to coconut oil), in your coffee. It adds fat to your coffee so you don't get the spike. However, I do recommend that you use Bulletproof Coffee in moderation. I am a fan, but use it in moderation.

The coconut oil fat has many health benefits for our brain. There have been numerous studies on dementia and Alzheimer's using coconut oil. Our brains are made up of a lot of fat. Feeding our brains with the good healthy fats may improve brain function.

Other things to avoid: chemical-laden household products and cleaners, and antibacterial soaps. We don't need antibacterial soaps. Warm water and regular soap do perfectly fine. You can find studies on the ingredients such as triclosan in antibacterial soaps and harmful cancer-causing effects linked to it. I wrote an article called "The Master Chemist," which has to do with using antibacterial soaps versus substances that have been used for thousands of years: traditional essential oils.

Exodus chapter 30 verse 25 says, "And shall make an oil of holy ointment, an ointment compound after the art of the apothecary. It shall be a holy anointing oil." Other things to look at avoiding are mainstream deodorant, lotions, and shampoos. Regarding antibacterial soaps, deodorants, lotions, and shampoos: get rid of the common versions of those as well. Most deodorants contain aluminum, which has been shown to increase the risk of Alzheimer's and other neurological conditions. The skin is the largest organ and covering the skin with all kinds of preservatives and chemicals can raise the risk of cancers and neurological conditions. They're just not needed. Replace them with natural options containing essential oils.

God is the Master Chemist. Antibiotics and antibacterials have only been on the scene for a little over a hundred years, and some not even that long. We're already seeing resistant superbugs such as MRSA, which have become resistant to these antibacterial soaps, creams, and cleaners. Yet the pathogens are still not resistant to the traditional essential oils that have been around thousands of years, such as tea tree oil. Essential oils contain several different compounds that the bug can't be resistant to. Only the Master Chemist can create something like that.

While we're on the subject of detoxification, I'll add negative thinking, news, mainstream news, TV, and most social media. Detoxing from them is beneficial.

Now the big one: many prescription and over the counter—medications. Try to eliminate or reduce those as much as you can. A disclaimer is necessary here. The statements I've been making have not been evaluated by the FDA and they're not intended to cure, diagnose, or treat any disease. You always should talk with your healthcare professional about these items. For many acute and rare conditions, you have to do mainstream medications and healthcare, but in my opinion, a lot of chronic conditions can be either eliminated or taken care of through the natural medicines that God created.

You say why over-the-counter medications? Aren't those safe? Why would they be available over-the-counter if they're not? One just needs to look at acetaminophen and all the liver toxicity it can cause, or ibuprofen and the stomach ulcers and kidney problems it can cause, for example. I am horrified that acid blockers—proton-pump inhibitors such as Prilosec and Prevacid—are on the market. It's just horrific to me that those are over-the-counter. Even now I see things such as nasal steroids. I have a friend who developed a severe case of cataracts and eye trouble from using a nasal steroid. It is now over-the-counter, available to everyone. Stay away from OTC and prescription medications if you can. There are natural anti-inflammatories, natural pain relievers, natural ways to prevent and reduce reflux and allergies. There's often no need for the manufactured versions.

Rules of Thumb on Elimination and Detox

1) If you can't pronounce it, don't use it. That's either internally or externally. For example, most maple syrups on the market don't even contain maple syrup. They contain so many artificial preservatives and flavors, but all they are is high fructose corn syrup with maple syrup flavoring and ingredients such as sodium hexametaphosphate. Is that what you want your small children to be ingesting? How about looking on a bottle of organic maple syrup? You know what will say as its ingredient? 100% organic maple syrup. If you can't pronounce it, don't use it.

2) Shop around the perimeter of the grocery store. Don't go down the aisles. Shop around the perimeter. That's where the produce is. That's where the meats are. Shop around the perimeter.

3) Try not to eat anything that comes in a box or a bag. One of the worst aisles in the grocery store is the breakfast and cereal aisle. Anything that's in a box, anything that's processed is going to contain many of the things I discussed—artificial sweeteners, artificial colors, artificial ingredients, preservatives. Stay away from them.

4) Replace sodas and artificially sweetened drinks with water, tea, or coffee. Now if you have to do some juice, it's okay sometimes, but if you would, dilute it with water and buy things that are 100% fruit juice. Read labels.

5) Be moderate. Don't torture yourself, such as being strict with yourself around the holidays. Give yourself treats and breaks. You don't have to do this 100%, and I don't do it 100%. That's how you can make it last. Around the holidays and when you're traveling, just do the best you can. One rule of thumb is to make the healthiest choice from what is in front of you. When you're on a trip or vacation, just make the healthiest choice from what is in front of you.

Detoxification is important and often overlooked. Here are five things that can help speed up detox out of your body.

1) Water. One thing I suggest: first thing in the morning, as soon as you wake up, go pour a glass of warm water. Make sure you're using filtered or purified water, not tap water. Put in a tablespoon or two of apple cider vinegar and a tablespoon or two of lemon juice. Drink that down really fast. It is a natural, easy cleansing and detox formula that is also antibacterial. It may help with constipation and acid reflux or heartburn. If you struggle with reflux or heartburn, do that mixture about 20 or 30 minutes before each meal.

2) Coconut oil. Taking a tablespoon or two of coconut oil a day will help eliminate a lot of bacteria and yeast in your body. Coconut oil is antibacterial, both topically and internally. A big caution with that is to start with it gradually. People who get into coconut oil too fast will find themselves spending too much time in the restroom, so take caution there.

3) Sweating. Matthew McConaughey said that he tries to sweat every day. You should do the same thing. Does that mean you're going to sweat every day? No, not every day, but it is a good idea to try to sweat every day. The skin is our largest organ. We get rid of a lot of toxins through sweating.

By the way, that includes sweating through the armpits. When you cover those with aluminum-laden deodorants, it keeps those toxins in you. Just keep that in mind. Is there a time and place for antiperspirants? Say you're going to a wedding or an event, or you're going to be speaking or doing something else where your appearance and grooming need to meet a particular standard. Is it okay to use antiperspirant/deodorant then? Yes, absolutely. But you don't have to use it all the time. Natural products containing essential oils are a better option than the common products.

4) Raw veggie and fruit juicing. This is an excellent way to detox your body really quickly. There are so many different formulas you can get. I do like the juicers that will allow the whole fruit to be pulverized (such as a Ninja or a NutriBullet) over the extractors

because you get the fiber along with the sugar that's in the juice. Raw fruit and veggie juicing can really radically change your life. If you've never seen the documentary *Fat, Sick, & Nearly Dead*, I highly recommend it.

5) Liver cleanses. You can do those seasonally. It's a good idea to do one every season. When I was working in the pharmacy, I took a herb called milk thistle every day to keep my liver cleansed. If you're working around fertilizers, pesticides, or other chemicals, you should probably be doing that all the time. As an added bonus, things such as seeds and nuts can help, because those add fiber and that helps get rid of toxins through your stool.

A note on water: Water must be pure. We don't get enough water. Most of us are walking around dehydrated. A good rule of thumb is to drink half an ounce to one ounce of water for each pound of body weight. A person who weighs 200 pounds needs to drink 100 to 200 ounces of water per day. I recommend drinking one ounce per pound, especially if you're active. For starters, aim for the middle. That would be 150 ounces a day for a 200-lb person. That's seven to eight 20-ounce bottles. Start with one 20-ounce bottle in the morning. Drink it, then, throughout the day, refill it from a five-gallon jug of purified water. There are different apps for tracking that. Some watches even track water consumption. Start tracking your water.

Drinks like coffee, tea, and alcohol cause your body to dehydrate, so you do need to replace every cup of caffeinated beverage or alcohol with a cup of water.

The Natural Pharmacist Chronic Condition Cure-all
Here are four things you could do that may eliminate a lot of chronic conditions, such as headaches, depression, foggy thinking, and many digestive disorders.

1) Pray. Invite others to pray for you as well. Be open and honest. The Bible says that we can confess to each other what we're struggling with and let others pray for us, and we can be healed.

2) Replace sodas and alcohol with water, but not the flavored, artificially sweetened water.

3) Eliminate foods such as artificial sweeteners, flavors, and colors; grains, and nitrates, which are preservatives found in a lot of processed deli meats.

4) Exercise.

Do those things for a month and see what happens. See if you don't get fewer migraine headaches. See if your mental focus and clarity don't reappear and see if your depression doesn't go away or at least lessen greatly. That's just a little natural pharmacist tip there for you.

Replenish

Now that we've eliminated some toxins, it's time to replenish or nourish. How do we do that? I've already mentioned some of these, but I'm going to mention them again. Water. Are you seeing a recurring theme here? Water, water, water. Other items that help replenish our body: juicing and healthy smoothies. That is great to do for breakfast every morning. You do not need to skip breakfast. It's the most important meal of your day. You need to get your day started on the right track. Having a protein-based smoothie with things such as flax seeds, chia seeds, coconut oil, and powdered greens gets the day started off on a solid nutritional foundation.

As far as diets, there are two I usually recommend. My number one for energy is the Paleo diet. Why Paleo? I was introduced to the Paleo diet through my relationship with Iron Tribe Fitness. If you want to perform at your peak, if you want to have the clearest thinking possible, Paleo is the way to go. Combining a Paleo diet and daily exercise is a powerful way to transform your health. Robb Wolf says, "The Paleo diet is the healthiest way you can eat because it is the only nutritional approach that works with your genetics to help you stay lean, strong, and energetic." He said, "Research in biology, biochemistry, ophthalmology, dermatology, and many other disciplines indicate it is our modern diet full of refined foods, trans fats, and sugar that is at the root of degenerative diseases such as obesity, cancer, diabetes, heart disease, Parkinson's, Alzheimer's, depression, and infertility.

What is a Paleo diet? Fruits, vegetables, lean meats, seafood, nuts and seeds, and healthy fats. What do you avoid? Dairy, grains, processed food, and sugars, legumes, starches, and alcohol. You may say "I can't do that. Where can I get ideas for meals?" You can go online and you can just Google Paleo diet and find all kinds of recipes and resources. My favorite recipe resource, though, is *emeals.com*. They provide a weeklong plan, complete with grocery list, and have options for an individual, a couple, or a family. They make it so easy, and the recipes are really great.

The other diet I highly recommend is the Mediterranean diet. It is a little bit more flexible and it allows some things such as red wine in moderation. It doesn't do as much red meat as you see in the Paleo diet. For overall health and longevity, I'm convinced that a Gluten Free Mediterranean Diet is the way to go.

This chart comparing a Paleo diet and a Mediterranean diet (*http://blog.emeals.com/comparing-paleo-clean-eating-and-mediterranean/*) comes from *emeals.com*. A Mediterranean diet has been proven to reduce the risk of dying from heart disease by 25 to 30%, and to decrease cancers. There have been studies done with as many as 7,000 people on a Mediterranean diet vs. a lowfat diet. By the way, on that note, if you still believe that a lowfat diet is the way to go, it's about time for you to put up your Tab soda and get out of the 80s, please. I beg you. That is known to be inaccurate. We actually need more fat. It just has to be the healthy fats.

The study that was done on 7,000 people on the Mediterranean diet vs. a lowfat diet was actually stopped early because the benefits were so clear. Not only did the people who were on a Mediterranean diet benefit, they were able to stick with it better than people could stick with a lowfat diet. The people on the lowfat diet couldn't stay on it. Why? Because it's miserable. Our bodies crave fats. Our brains are made up of fat. Fat is fuel. That's why people couldn't stay on it.

With diets, I recommend shooting for 75%, which means three out of every four meals. You can go 100%, but I'm telling you that you'll stay on it and it will become more of a lifestyle if you'll shoot for 75%. That's three out of every four meals. That way you're not beating yourself up, not throwing your hands up in the air and giving up when you do cheat. I may do a six- to eight-meal run of all Paleo. Then on a weekend, all three of my meals one day may be total trash. But of course, I always keep in mind trying to make the next healthiest choice that is in front of me. Go organic and fresh whenever possible. Whenever you can, go organic and fresh from your local farmer's market. The nutrient content is higher and the toxin content lower in those foods.

Have treats every so often. Now, if you know you are addicted to something such as sugar if you can't control yourself, then you need to eliminate it just like an alcoholic eliminates alcohol. But if you can, give yourself a treat. I'm a huge fan of ice cream. When my family travels, we love to stop and get ice cream. It's okay.

Although people try to eat well, we can no longer get enough nutrients for our bodies through eating alone, so supplementation is necessary. It's recommended for us to have five servings of fruits and vegetables every day. I would be willing to bet most of us are not consistently getting that many. If you're not, you're deficient.

What do we supplement? I have a top five list to recommend:

- A good quality multivitamin, perhaps specific for your gender and age.
- A probiotic, which is the healthy bacteria that has been shown to be beneficial for everything from our digestive health to our immune system, to our brain, to our skin.

- Omega-3 (a good fat), which is found in high-quality, mercury-free distilled fish oils. If you're a vegan, then use flax oil.
- Vitamin D. Vitamin D is beneficial for everything from bone health to immune health to prevention of breast and prostate cancer. It's also a natural antidepressant. Many of us are deficient in vitamin D.

Also, an herbal adaptogen, such as Siberian ginseng or rhodiola or ashwagandha may be helpful to you. Adaptogens are amazing. The reason why they're called adaptogens is they adapt to our body. Some people experience fatigue in response to stress. People get worn out. Some have problems sleeping during stress, because too much cortisol keeps a person hyped up and unable to calm down. Adaptogens have an amazing ability to regulate and normalize the body's response to stress. I like Siberian ginseng, but it can raise the blood pressure a little bit. In that case, rhodiola is a great safe choice. All of these have to be top-quality nutritional supplements. The next five I would recommend:
- Curcumin
- Grape seed extract or resveratrol
- Coenzyme Q10
- Magnesium, and
- Olive leaf extract, along with those above.

What else do we supplement? If you're exercising, which I hope by now you're convinced you need to be doing, you should get a good preworkout beverage or mix, a good recovery drink, and a good high-quality protein to supplement. Now keep in mind you've got to look for what I cautioned earlier: artificial sweeteners, preservatives, and flavors. Good-quality natural sports nutrition is paramount.

You can supplement for different things as varied as stress, sleep, memory improvement, and digestion (which is a huge issue), as well as for your immune system and inflammation. While we're on that note, as far as helpful nutrition for conditions, I'm going to mention prescription drugs again. What people don't realize is the depletions that many prescription drugs cause in the body. Have you ever seen the movie *European Vacation*? There's a scene in there called "Big Ben, Parliament." I recommend it. They get caught in the roundabout, and for hours, he's going around saying, "See kids, Big Ben, Parliament, Big Ben, Parliament."

The same thing happens to us when we get on prescription medications, which deplete nutrients. I call it the vicious drug roundabout or the vicious drug cycle. What happens is we take a prescription medication for something such as reflux, a medication that's not meant to be used more than a month or six weeks, and we take it for years. That medication depletes acid out of our stomach, which causes us to not absorb nutrients like we should. Our stomachs are meant to be more acidic. The change causes the depletion of vitamin B12 and magnesium in our bodies. Both are critical for brain health, memory, and thinking. Magnesium is nature's own muscle relaxant. Being depleted of magnesium can cause everything from restless leg syndrome to migraine headaches to mitral valve prolapse.

Then we start getting migraine headaches. Now it could be caused by a little bit of artificial sweeteners or stress, but then we end up on a migraine medication or we end up on something for restless leg syndrome (which is actually an antiParkinson's drug being used for restless legs), when something like magnesium can easily fix it. We think to ourselves, *I'm just getting older. I guess it's normal just to feel bad, to feel this way.* No, it's your medications. You see what I'm talking about, how this happens? It's very, very common. Be very wary of your prescription drugs and aware of the nutrients that they are depleting.

That ends the section on nourishing our body. Now let's talk about nourishing our mind. Romans 12:2 says, "Don't copy the behavior and customs of this world, but let God transform you into a new person by changing the way you think" (NLT). How is your thinking?

"The Electron"

"The Electron" was a nickname given to me by my friends early on in my career because of my negative thinking and my tendency to complain. An electron has a negative charge. My nature has been to be negative. I've had to really work at this over the years. That's why I developed this system to work on my thinking and help you improve your thinking as well. Let me give you five ways to improve your thinking.

1) Reduce your exposure to worldly thinking. That would be TV, negative music, inappropriate websites, news, especially the gossip news where people are yelling at each other and talking about other people, reality TV shows (which in my opinion are nothing but gossip and slander), and even social media. There's negative talk all over social media. Have you ever tried a media fast? I recommend you do that. Or how about a social media fast? Try it for a week. You know what? I don't watch the news. You can still get your news by talking to people. You're going to find out pretty much anything that goes on. If it really matters, you're going to hear about it.

2) Increase your "Vitamin Bs" from the learning chapter. Those are the Bible, books, and blogs. Go back to the learning chapter if you need to.

3) Increase your vitamin E, which is encouragement. Fill your mind with positive messages, encouraging music. I recommend Christian music. When you hear a song you like, download that song. Get on apps such as music streaming stations. I love stations such as WAYFM. When you hear a song you like, which really speaks to you, download that song and put it on a playlist for those mornings when you don't feel like exercising, or for Fridays when

you're worn down. Also, include encouraging podcasts and positive books.

4) Exercise. It really changes your mindset. If you push through an exercise when you're having a tough time, you're going to feel accomplished. Like the SEC commissioner said, "You're going to feel like you've already got a win for the day." Even if it's just walking for five minutes while listening to encouraging music or the Bible, do some. I recommend the book of Psalms because it is encouraging.

5) Stay busy. Now, this may seem to contradict some things I'm going to say about resting because entrepreneurs and business owners never tend to rest enough. There is a time for both. Stay busy with your morning routine, which is self-care, nourishment, exercise, and spending time with God and family. Then focus on your to-do list and your work. Then, at the end of the day, get back to your family. Stay involved and connected to your family. Be present with them. If you stay busy with all these things, you won't have time to fill your mind with bad things like TV and bad websites. Do take clarity breaks, though, and do rest on days that you need to rest. God made the Sabbath day for a reason.

Rest and Relaxation

Those things should help you with your thoughts. You have to take time to recover from your exercise, from your work, from the mental stress. I like to call Sabbaths free days, which was given to me by a man named Dan Sullivan of The Strategic Coach. Those are days that you spend where you do no work. You answer no emails. You will find that you become more energized and creative when you do that. I did a podcast about that once, which is called "Rest or Die." (*http://www.stephenfskinner.com/episode-014-rest-or-die/*)

Another beneficial key thing for the mind is to laugh. Proverbs 17:22 says, "A cheerful heart is good medicine." Laugh. Laugh at yourself, number one. Don't take yourself so seriously. I love what Jim Valvano said in his Espy speech: "I just got one last thing. I urge all of you to enjoy your life, the precious moments you have, to spend each day with some laughter and some thought, to get your emotions going." What a great quote that was.

Finally, play. Go have some fun before it's too late. Memories matter more than home theaters do. You're choosing how to spend your money. Spend it on memories instead of material things that are going to waste away. Go travel. Do things with your family. Get outside, please. God's given us this wonderful world to explore. Go outside and enjoy it. This is a big reason for exercise and why it's so important to take care of your body, so you can go do these things. It's important to have the ability to go make memories. That's what's going to last—not the TV, not the car.

As far as taking time to nourish yourself, to go through this process, you're probably having some doubts. But you need to discover your "why." What is your "why?"

The Real Reason Why

When I talk about nourishing, does it mean that I always do this perfectly? No, I'm not perfect, but I do intentionally schedule and work on myself to get better. I want you to as well. Until your "why" becomes big enough or serious enough, you're not going to make these changes that last. My question to you is when will your "why" be big enough? Are you going to wait until you're in an ER with massive chest pains and your spouse and your children are outside, scared to death? Are you going to wait until you're sitting in a doctor's office and you've been told you have cancer or diabetes? "Here's a prescription for a shot you're going to have to give yourself every day. By the way, it usually costs around $500 a month."

Are you going to wait until that? Or are you going to wait until your child says, "Daddy, why are you always so grumpy and tired? You never want to play with me. All you do is sit in front of the TV and yell at it, or you sleep all the time" or your child says, "Mommy, why do you sleep all the time? Why do you act so sad all the time?" Are you going to wait for that? Maybe you're going to wait until an employer says, "We're going to have to cut your hours. Your attitude and your productivity have fallen too much." Or perhaps someone working for you says, "I'm going to this other company because this is just not a good environment for me."

Have you ever been to the point where everything seems to be caving in on you at work or at home, or everything was going wrong and you just feel like you can't do anymore? Have you ever felt like you're getting nowhere like you almost can't breathe from overwhelming stress, weight, and pressure? I've been there. That's when I finally discovered that I had to change. Now I've made it how I live. I hope you are making it how you live, too. Now, every day, we are working at praying and praising, listening to God and learning something, taking action and nourishing our spirit, body, and mind. It's time to start being thankful every day.

Chapter 8—Thankfulness

"Be thankful in all circumstances, for this is God's will for you who belong to Christ Jesus" 1 Thessalonians 5:18 (NLT).

"For the despondent, every day brings trouble; for the happy heart, life is a continual feast" Proverbs 15:15 (NLT).

"This is the day the Lord has made. I will rejoice and be glad in it!" Psalm 118:24 (NLT).

"You have surrounded me on every side, behind me and before me, and You have placed Your hand gently on my shoulder. It is the most amazing feeling to know how deeply You know me, inside and out; the realization of it is so great that I cannot comprehend it" Psalm 139:5–6 (The Voice).

"But thanks be to God, who gives us the victory through our Lord Jesus Christ" 1 Corinthians 15:57.

"An attitude of gratitude before the Lord is one he will always honor."—Buck Jacobs

In the chapter on action, I told you about my miracle pill. Here is another miracle pill for you, one that has been scientifically proven to do all these things:
- bring you more business, friends, opportunities, and wealth
- improve overall physical health (reduce headaches, aches, and pains, increase exercise frequency, which also improves health)
- improve mental health (detoxes envy, resentment, and guilt)
- reduce road rage and temper

- help you sleep better
- improve self-esteem thereby decreasing depression, and
- improve resilience or grit

Imitate Grandma Skinner

First Corinthians 11:1 (NLT) says, "You should imitate me, just as I imitate Christ." I say you should imitate Grandma Skinner, just as she imitates Christ. Why do I say that? Grandma Skinner, Dorothy Skinner, is 99 years old at the writing of this book. She is in a nursing home, in a little room, stuck in a corner.

Almost always, I go visit her thinking that's it's going to do her a lot of good. It's going to cheer her up. What does she do every time I go? She flips it back on me! She turns what I think it will be like— me blessing her—into her blessing me. She does that because she's so full of gratitude and joy for anybody who comes to see her, or anything anyone gives her. She truly is the most thankful person, the most loving person, the most joyful person, of anyone I've ever met.

Every morning, when we wake up, we have a choice to have either an abundance mindset or a scarcity mindset. In the last chapter, I talked about my nature, which was to be negative, to have a scarcity mindset, to think the world is against me. Often, I do still wake up with this mindset, just thinking the world's against me. I know where that comes from, the Enemy. Competing as an independent pharmacy against the big-box chain stores had a part to play in it. I believe, also, it was just my nature.

In the business coaching I do, we have a tool where we craft the client's core focus, also known as a mission statement. Jesus gave us his in one sentence. It's pretty clear what that is. In John 10:10, he said, "I have come that they may have life and have it more abundantly."

Before he said that, in that same Scripture (verse 5), he also said, "The thief comes only to steal, kill and destroy." Okay. The thief comes to steal what? How about your joy, how about your energy?

What about your self-esteem? Kill what? Maybe it's your goals; maybe it's what God created you to do on this earth. Maybe it's your willpower. Maybe it's your unique ability that you were created to use. Destroy what? How about your relationships, your dreams, or even your health? That's what this book's about: fighting against the Enemy's theft and destruction.

You're reading this, and you're saying, "Uh-oh. I was afraid he was going to go there. The prosperity gospel." No, not completely. There is no doubt this world is tough. Life is tough. Running a business, an organization, or even a family is tough. Jesus himself also said, in John 16:33, "I've told you these things so that in me you may have peace, because in this world you will have trouble, but take heart. I have overcome the world."

Look at this verse again, John 10:10 (ESV). "I've come here that they may have *life* and have it more *abundantly*." As Matthew Hartsfield of Van Dyke Church in Tampa, Florida, says, "Did he say, 'I've come to give you life and a life full of averages, averageness?' No. Did he say, 'I've come to give you life and a life full of boredom?' No. 'I've come to give you life and a life full of shame, guilt, and misery?' No. Jesus said, 'My mission is to give you Life.'" LIFE. What is that? That's eternal life and it's life in all of its fullness. That's abundance. What is abundance? That's growth—as this book, as this system suggests, 100X growth.

What limits our growth? Well, let's look at this parable. The parable that this book is based on is the parable of the soil. Perhaps we have worries, troubles, no roots, no depth to our soil. If you go back and read that in Luke 8, you'll see that it's the hard ground that doesn't allow deep roots and it's the worries and cares of the world, the thorns, which limit our growth. Ray Edwards said, "I'm always a little amused when I hear a criticism leveled at those of us who believe God intended men to prosper and be in good health. Especially when it sounds like this. 'Oh, so you believe in the prosperity gospel.' The term itself is used with derision. Another form of this question is, 'Don't tell me you're one of those health-and-wealth gospel believers.' I always want to reply, 'Would you prefer a sickness and poverty gospel? Do you think Jesus came not to give us life and more abundantly, but rather sickness and death more quickly?'"

How do we flip this mindset from scarcity to abundance, from negative thinking to positive? Like I said, it is a choice. Sometimes we wake up with this negative mindset, and that doesn't come from God. I hope it's pretty clear to you. It is a choice. Well, this is how we do it: **gratitude**. What is gratitude? Gratitude is being thankful, first to God, and then to others.

Nothing can transform your mind and your thoughts more profoundly than gratitude can. Gratitude is being thankful no matter what. Norman Vincent Peal said, "Gratitude recharges the soul. Anyone who is grateful is focusing on what is good. Ultimately, all good things come from God. This means the thankful person is aligning himself with the most powerful force in the universe and is drawing strength from it. Gratitude is focusing on what you already have that we so often take for granted, versus focusing on what we don't have."

One time a man went to a church. A woman there approached him with a smile and said, "What's wrong?"

The man said, "I need money. I just don't have any money for gas." He was just so distraught over everything.

"Okay, well, how did you get here?"

He said, "Well, my car."

She goes, "Well, thank the Lord you have a car to drive. It's cold outside, isn't it?"

"Yes," he replied.

"I see you have a coat."

"Yes, I do."

She asked, "Isn't it wonderful that you have a coat in this cold weather?" The point that she was making to this man comes from Philippians 4:4–8 (ESV). It says, "Rejoice in the Lord *always*. Again, I say, rejoice. Let your reasonableness be known to everyone.

The Lord is at hand. Don't be anxious about anything," (such as the gas) "but in everything, by prayer and supplication with thanksgiving, let your request be known to God. The peace of God, which surpasses all understanding, will guard your hearts and your minds, in Christ Jesus. Finally, brothers, whatever's true, whatever's honorable, whatever's just, whatever's pure, whatever is lovely, whatever is commendable; if there's any excellence, if there's anything worthy of praise, think about these things."

It was Paul who wrote that from the dungeon, and what he's saying is to ask properly. Make sure you first say, "Lord, I'm so thankful for this. These clothes I do have. I'm thankful for this job I do have. I'm thankful for the money that I do have, the food I do have, but Lord, can you help me with some more so I can . . ." Approaching it from that standpoint is what this Scripture is talking about.

Gratitude is easier said than done. Good examples can help. I can't tell you how often, especially after leaving my Grandmother Skinner, I'll say, "I want to be like her: a person of joy, a person who makes a difference in others' lives, so they can see a joy that can't be explained. I want to be a person who makes people glad to be around me."

It takes work. It has to become a habit, but it can only become a habit with this daily discipline. Once you do this, you will create more abundance, more prosperity, more well-being and happiness than you could ever imagine. How do we do this? Well, number one, you've got to be willing to accept Christ as your Lord and spend time with him as a part of this PLANTing process. Especially the *P* and *L*, praise, prayer, listening, and learning. Remember, we're working on our soil here, trying to make it fertile for growth.

Look at what Paul said in Colossians 2:6–7, "And now, just as you accepted Christ Jesus as your Lord, you must continue to follow him. Let your roots grow down into him and let your lives be built on him. Then your faith will grow strong in the truth you were taught and you will **overflow with thankfulness**." Then he also said (in

Ephesians 3:20) that God is "able to do immeasurably more than all we ask or imagine, according to his power that is at work within us."

Accept him as Lord and be thankful that he saved you. Start every day with prayer. If you do this daily, it's going to happen. Some days, by spending time with him, you're going to be overwhelmed with what he's done for you.

The second way is through gratitude journaling. Why journaling? Journaling does several things. It helps you retain what you've read by listening to and spending time with him. It changes your perspective, and it helps you focus. It helps you set and track your goals, and measure your progress. What gets measured gets paid attention to. It's just a fact. Journaling also helps boost your self-confidence and helps you become open and honest. In my business coaching, that's one of the core things I stress: you have to be open and honest with your team or your mastermind group. We're not going to get anywhere unless we're open and honest. Journaling helps start that process.

Journaling is like looking at yourself in the mirror. So many times I've started my day writing in my journal, "I'm overwhelmed" or "I feel frustrated" or "I'm tired." That's me being open and honest and vulnerable before the Lord. Also, journaling opens our hearts to receive his Word.

James 1:22–25 says, "Do not merely listen to the Word and so deceive yourself. Do what it says. Anyone who listens to the Word, but does not do it as it says is like someone who looks at his face in the mirror, and after looking at himself, goes away and immediately forgets what he looks like. But whoever looks intently into the perfect law that gives freedom, and continues in it, not forgetting what they've heard, *but doing it*, they will be *blessed* in what they do." That's one reason journaling helps.

Journaling helps you to record any ideas and promptings you receive, so you can share them and affect the lives of others. Habakkuk 2:2 (NLT) says, "Then the LORD said to me, 'Write my answer plainly on tablets, so that a runner can carry the correct message to others.'"

Journaling also helps to humble us. That is the key to transformation. Listen to the importance of being humble in Proverbs 3:5–6 . "Trust in the Lord with all your heart. Lean not on your own understanding. In all your ways, submit to him and he will make your path straight." Notice submit comes first. We want all these answers when we come before the Lord on a daily basis, but we're not willing to submit first. Right?

Those are some of the reasons why journaling is so important. It lets you be humble, open and honest, and vulnerable; and it helps you track your goals and your progress.

Darren Hardy said, "To help you become aware of your choices, I want you to track every action that relates to the area of your life that you want to improve." That's from his book, *The Compound Effect*. He says, "Tracking is my go-to transformation model for everything that ails me."

Journal first thing in the morning. I keep repeating that, I know. You heard that early on in this book, but it's so important. Why first thing in the morning? Lamentations 3:22–23 (ESV), says, "The steadfast love of the Lord never ceases. His mercies never come to an end. They are *new every morning*. Great is your faithfulness." Please start this in the morning.

I once saw a video which conveyed that on the eighth day, God created dogs for our enjoyment. Well, I believe on the eighth day, God created morning time with coffee, birds, and sunrises, along with dogs. Those are some of the great joys of life to me. There's nothing like sitting with a cup of fresh warm coffee on a cool morning, looking out over the earth while becoming more alert and hearing the birds. It's just so special. Every day, I open up my journal and write three things that I'm thankful for. This is the gratitude journal that I'm talking about. I start by saying either, "Thank you, Father," or "Blessings in my life," and I'll list three things. I learned this from Buck Jacobs, who I've mentioned before in this book.

Those three things can be something as small as, "Thank you for this cup of coffee." What I want you to do is try to remember anything good that happened in that last 24 hours. Maybe you had a positive conversation with someone you're trying to make a deal with. Perhaps you just had a nice lunch with your spouse. Maybe you had a great conversation with a coworker. Perhaps your kid just gave you a big hug, or you're proud of something your child did. Maybe you're thankful for your wife. Often, I'll just be thankful for God's Word. Write three things that you're thankful for, first thing.

It's amazing how often I'll wake up tired, frustrated, or just angry at the world like I mentioned before. These five minutes—which are all it takes to do that—can change everything. Now your heart is thankful and humble because you have considered the blessings you've been given. You're ready to receive the Lord's Word, which is the Prayer and Listen part that comes next.

I know those chapters came before this in the book, but I do want you to start this first. I just did that so it would be easy to remember, but I do want you to start this process first. Here are some things I've written down in my journal before, as a thank you. "Got a new tenant. Got a new client or a new member. A new prospect. Had a good conversation with . . . Ran into . . . Our mastermind meeting was great. So-and-so mentioned a book that sounds great. Can't wait to get that."

You may be saying, "That's good, but I can't think of anything." Well, start simple. Like I said, start with, "My daughter looked so cute, yesterday, in her outfit. Or, "My spouse was so unselfish to . . ." "Had a great lunch with . . ." "It was such a pretty day . . ." "I noticed . . ." "Ran into (fill in the blank)." "Was good to see . . ." I've said before, "It's cold and rainy, but here I am with a warm cup of coffee and shelter. I can't believe I get to spend this time with you, my Creator, alone. Yesterday was tough, but I really love what

I'm doing now. I'm so thankful for . . ." I've written this one many times: "Went to see Grandma, she cheered us up so much. She . . ."

I want you to go get a copy of My Best Day Ever journal template (*the100xlife.com/journal*). What I use is an app called Day One (*http://dayoneapp.com/*). You don't have to use an app. I love Day One because it's saved in the cloud. You can add pictures to it. It automatically records the time, date, and even the weather and your location when you wrote that entry. It becomes your life, laid out.

A simple notebook will do. The journal is a resource you can print and use to do your journaling on one side and make your to-do list on the other side. I've done that before. Or you can do it all on Day One and then print it out and take that with you for the day. The point is, do it how you want to. You don't have to spend money on this. You can take my template, print it out, and you're ready to go. Okay?

I always do gratitude first. Then I open up Daily Audio Bible and a Bible app and start listening and reading along. Then, in my Bible app, I highlight verses as I go. Once I finish the reading, I go back through the Scripture I've highlighted, and then I copy that. Then I paste those Scriptures into my Day One app, along with my thoughts and my notes. It starts out as blessings or the three things that I'm thankful for.

Then I'll write, "God told me today . . ." Then I'll put the Scripture, thoughts, what he's saying to me under there. Then after I get finished, I go back and reread my journal. I ask God, "What are you saying to me?" I'll even pray it back to him in the form of a prayer, starting with being thankful. When was the last time you prayed to God, just thanking him? We often pray to God asking for this or that, but we don't spend time talking to him and just being thankful. We're his children. If you have a child, don't you love it when your child just tells you thank you?

I have a son who has a lot of gratitude. He's constantly telling us that he loves us and it means so much when you hear that versus all the time hearing, "Can I have, can I have? I want, I want." It's the same thing with our Lord. He wants to have a relationship with us. He knows our heart but he wants to hear us say it. That's the purpose of gratitude.

That's how I pray, with thankfulness for the blessings. I go through the verses. Some of the verses are praises, some are convictions, and some are repentance. Then, and only then, do I add my personal requests. Prayer is a daily conversation with God. Don't just end it there. Add personal requests from friends, other people you know, things going on in the world, decisions you have to make, and wisdom you need to come to your awareness. You can bring those requests before him. Then I end with telling him I love him and we continue to talk through the rest of the day like I mentioned in Chapter 4. You can do the same.

We have ways to be thankful:

1) Have gratitude. Do that by accepting Christ, if you haven't already. Spend time with him every day.

2) Journal

3) Act on that gratitude. Share the love, I like to say. With whom? First, with God, through praise and prayer; then with others.

At any time, if you feel a blast of appreciation or a sudden surge of gratitude, translate that into action. How? Write that note. Send out a text to somebody. How about a written "thank you" note, which is a lost art? That can go a long way.

The other day a man told me he got a "thank you" note in the mail. That day, he said, he probably got 100 emails. He didn't open every one of them, but he got one "thank you" note, and it got a 100% open rate. Those notes will get opened; they will make a difference. It is said that the written note triggers a different part of our brain. It triggers a more emotional response than a digital note does. We know that's true. Take the time to do that. It can make a huge difference.

If you don't have time for that, like I said, just send a text. Send an email, make a phone call. Leave someone a voice mail: "Hey, I was just thinking about you. I'm so thankful for this about you." Or even share what you're thankful for on social media. I often will catch a great sunrise, and it's amazing how often I'll catch a sunrise on the same day that I read a Psalm or something talking about how amazing the Lord is, and then I'll throw that together and share that on social media.

How about just thanking your people and showing appreciation for them? I did a podcast episode on that, which you may want to check out, about a cheap, easy way to retain your employees. It's about showing gratitude. Send that small gift; send those flowers. This has to do with acting, putting this into *action*. Act as if this impulse you received were a divine command. *You know why? Because it is.* That will become more and more evident as you go through this daily process of listening, spending time, and being thankful. As we put this practice of gratitude and thankfulness in place, it will slowly start to change our attitude. As I said at the beginning, this is a choice.

As a result of doing this, it's so much easier to choose a happy and positive attitude of abundance. John Maxwell said, "Happiness cannot be won, bought, or brought to you by another person. Rather, it results from a conscious choice to be grateful for our blessings and to make the best of life's letdowns. Whatever happens to us, we always have control over one thing. Our attitude." That's so true, isn't it? Also, I'm reminded of Jim Valvano. In his Espy speech, less than two months from his death, he said, "Cancer can take away all of my physical abilities. It cannot touch my mind, it cannot touch my heart, and it cannot touch my soul."

You've got to accept this, believe this. You weren't created to be nothing, you were meant for greatness. He came to give us the abundant life. You just need some dirt work, just like I. My hope and prayer is that you'll put this into practice and watch what happens.

You'll put this whole process of PLANTing, every day, into practice, and see what happens.

Why is it important? Because you're important. We're counting on you.

If you feel inadequate, if you feel you're not important, repeat these words out loud, after me.

"I have been crucified with Christ and I no longer live, but Christ lives in me. The life I now live in the body, I live by faith in the Son of God, who loved me and gave himself for me." Galatians 2:20.

"Our deepest fear is not that we are inadequate. Our deepest fear is that we are powerful beyond measure. It is our light, not our darkness, that most frightens us.

We ask ourselves, "Who am I to be brilliant, gorgeous, talented, fabulous?" Actually, who are you NOT to be? You are a child of God. Your playing small does not serve the world. There is nothing enlightened about shrinking so that other people won't feel insecure around you.

We are born to make manifest the glory of God that is within us. It is not just in some of us, it is in every one. And as we let our light shine, we give others permission to do the same. As we are liberated from our fears our presence liberates others."—Marianne Williamson

Perhaps you are thinking, "Stephen, do you actually do all this right away, first thing in the morning, or does it just need to happen by the time you go to bed at night? When do you actually do each of these segments?"

I do most of them first thing in the morning, and there are a few you *must* do first thing in the morning, but you will find a checklist in chapter two, and as long as you get them done, go for it! I do realize we are all different, and some have more time for themselves at night. The important thing for some of these is to do them with your daddy, your Father in Heaven. He wants some one-on-one time with you, and he is going to bring you amazing peace, joy, love, comfort, and even challenges to your life that you've never imagined! His masterpiece will start to become chiseled from that rock.

A big concern I have is if you wait until the end of the day with these, then the day is already gone, so please keep that in mind, as well as the example we see in Scripture as well as in our secular lives, from some of the best leaders of all time.

Before the world wakes up is the best time to do a lot of these, perhaps including exercising; but everybody is different. Some people would rather exercise late in the day. I'm not saying you have to do all of them in the morning. Sometimes I may listen or read in the evening as well.

Will your life change overnight? No. It takes a while. It is a slow process; so is farming. But like a plant, you will shortly begin to see stems, then buds. You will notice you are sleeping better, you are handling stress better, and maybe the headaches, joint aches, reflux, and constipation are improving. It might be a little thing here and there that you notice. You write it down in your gratitude journal. Then, you go back to Scripture. I encourage you to look at that Scripture I mentioned at the start. Look at those things and set those as your North Star to look at and you'll notice after a certain time, things change. For each of us, it may be different because we are all struggling with different things. For me, exercise is a huge factor that gives me peace and allows me to rest well at night. After I miss a few days (see, I'm not perfect, please do not think I believe I am!), I revert right back to the old Stephen: grumpy, stressed, and unable to sleep. If you don't believe me, ask my wife!

I know as you try to figure out how to do this system, there are going to be challenges. You are going to have struggles. In fact, I am willing to bet you may have more. How do I know this? It has been that way for others, including me, and you are starting a process of growing closer to God and becoming all he created you to be. The Enemy hates this; he wants you to not make an impact. Keep this in mind as you go through the journey.

This completes our PLANTing section of the book. Congratulations! You now know what you need to do to start producing the 100X Life! Now, like any good farmer, we get to celebrate the harvest and then start enjoying its FRUIT. Let's continue on, to see what that's going to look like.

Part 2—FRUIT

Just as PLANT is an acronym, so is FRUIT. In brief:

Freedom
Results
Unity
Impact
Transformation

Let's begin with an understanding of freedom, the *F* in FRUIT.

Chapter 9—Freedom

*"But the Fruit of the Spirit is love, joy, peace, patience, kindness, goodness, faithfulness, gentleness, self-control; against such things, **there is no law** Galatians 5:22–23 (ESV).*

*"So Christ has truly set us **free**. Now make sure that you **stay free**, and don't get tied up again in slavery to the law"* Galatians 5:1 (NLT).

*"For you have been called to live in **freedom**, my brothers and sisters. But don't use your **freedom** to satisfy your sinful nature. Instead, use your **freedom** to serve one another in love"* Galatians 5:13 (NLT).

*"So now there is no condemnation for those who belong to Christ Jesus. And because you belong to him, the power of the lifegiving Spirit has **freed** you from the power of sin that leads to death"* Romans 8:1–2 (NLT).

*"For this is the will of God, that by doing good you should put to silence the ignorance of foolish people. Live as people who are **free**, not using your **freedom** as a coverup for evil, but living as servants of God"* 1 Peter 2:15–16 (ESV).

Definition of ***FREEDOM***:

   1: the quality or state of being free: as
   a: the absence of necessity, coercion, or constraint in choice or action
   b: liberation from slavery or restraint or from the power of another: independence

Freedom has become my passion. This is my "why." For so long, I felt trapped behind the prescription counter, behind a business that was running me instead of me running it. I desired freedom more than anything. I was already successful. I was making plenty of money, but I had very little freedom. This is why I coach business owners to help them get what they want from their businesses. I help entrepreneurs, business owners, and directors of organizations. I use a complete set of simple tools that gets their people 100% on the same page, which is so key. Those tools, when implemented, give the leader the freedom to get what they want out of their business. It's a great thing to witness.

Freedom is one of the fruits that will be in this harvest. Freedom from what?

- freedom from stress and anxiety
- freedom from negative self-talk
- freedom from worrying about what others think. We can now make fun and laugh at ourselves because we're not taking ourselves so seriously.
- freedom from greed
- freedom from jealousy
- freedom from isolation
- freedom from being offended
- freedom from addictions
- freedom from some health problems
- freedom from medications, possibly
- freedom from fear
- freedom from shame. We're going to forget the past.
- freedom from past failures, and even freedom from past successes
- freedom, ultimately, from the fear of death

We will become freer from those things as we evolve with this process. What about freedom to? Freedom to be content, to trust, to love, to be open and honest, to be humble. We can be free to allow others to "sharpen our iron," to confess our weaknesses to others, and allow God to work his strength in our weaknesses. Second Corinthians 12:9–10 (NLT) says, "Each time he said 'my grace is all you need and my power works best in weakness.' So now I am glad to boast about my weaknesses so that the power of Christ can work through me. That's why I take pleasure in my weaknesses, and in the insults, hardships, persecutions, and troubles that I suffer for Christ, for when I am weak, then I am strong." It's freeing to give it to him.

What other things can we have freedom to do? To be bold, to forgive, to fail, and to give because we now have that abundance mindset that we talked about in the thankfulness chapter. We can have freedom to let go of the wheel and to realize who owns our business, who owns our organization, who is really in control. Let me tell you, there's great freedom there.

Second Timothy 1:7 says we can have freedom to feel powerful. We can have freedom to live in the moment, to be in the present, to stop worrying about the past or the future, and to enjoy the day for what it is: a gift. There is a freedom to be who you are, who God created you to be. If you're not sure what that is, there are different tests you can take which point to strengths and spiritual gifts.

You may enjoy the freedom to be like a child and be in awe and wonder. My favorite age of children is kindergarten age. The belief and the wonder regarding things such as Christmastime are so fun to see. Somewhere along the line we lose that. I don't ever want to lose that. I want to always be in awe and wonder. I think there are some things that we're never going to figure out in this life. Instead of trying to figure it out, let's just be in awe and wonder of it, and look forward to that day when we can find it all out. That is freedom. I hope you are finding that as well. Now let's move to the next fruit of the harvest: *R* for Results.

Chapter 10—Results

"For we are God's masterpiece. He has created us anew in Christ Jesus, so we can do the good things he planned for us long ago" Ephesians 2:10 (NLT).

God wants you to be productive. He wants his masterpiece to shine, to do excellent work. After all, it's all for his glory, as we read in 1 Corinthians 10:31. As you implement this daily system, his masterpiece will begin to become chiseled from that block of stone into the perfect person he created for his good works. Romans 12:11 says, "Never be lazy, but work hard and serve the lord enthusiastically." Colossians 3:23 (NLT) says, "Work willingly at whatever you do as though you are working for the Lord rather than for people." That is doing excellent work and getting excellent results. Titus 3 verse 14 says, "Our people must learn to devote themselves to doing what is good in order to provide for urgent needs and not live unproductive lives." Finally, Hebrews 11:6 (NLT) says, "And it's impossible to please God without faith. Anyone who wants to come to him must believe that God exists and that he rewards those who sincerely seek him."

With all that in mind, with this routine and practice, you're going to get incredible results. This is where the supernatural and the natural come together to produce this 100X Life harvest mentioned in Luke 8:8: "Why? Because action always creates results." No action = no results.

What are some results that you're going to experience? One would be more focus. You're going to have more mental clarity. If you exercise and implement the practices of the Paleo diet or the Mediterranean diet, you are going to notice your mind becoming clearer. If you're able to get off of some of your prescription medications or artificial sweeteners, you're going to notice an even clearer mind.

More important: you're going to experience clarity and more focus from God speaking to you every day. You're going to know what he wants from you. You're going to have more results because you're going to have that to-do list you're working on every day. Will you get everything done on that is your to-do list? No, you won't, but having that every day, setting that agenda, will allow more results to come into your life.

You're going to get more done. You're going to be doing as John Wooden said, making each day your masterpiece. Wisdom and knowledge are going to open up so many opportunities for you. It's really going to be amazing. You're also going to have more energy.

If you're able to sleep better, exercise, have better nutrition and take supplements, then you're going to have more energy. Using those things well will equal greater results.

Will this result in more income, more wealth, more abundance? Possibly, but there's no guarantee of that, and I'm not guaranteeing that. But let me ask you this: What are your health, wisdom, and peace worth? Like I said before, does wealth really matter if you're too sick to do anything with it? Jesus didn't promise us material wealth or earthly power, or even pleasure. He did guarantee true riches stored up in Heaven if we invest in the right things.

As a result of this process, you're also going to love him more. You're going to fall in love with him. As a result of falling in love with him, you're going to want to do more for him. That's going to produce results. You're just going to want to do more, and it's so much easier to do things out of love and gratitude than by "obligation or duty." That is why Jesus basically said, "Look, all you gotta do is Love me more than *anything*, with all your heart, and love my other perfect creations, my other children who I put you here to deal with (Matthew 22:37–38). He also essentially said, "Come here, let me take this for you, because when you let me, man, it will be easy, easy like Sunday morning . . ." (Commodores flashback). I love this version of his promise in Matthew 11:28–30 of The Message (MSG): "Are you tired? Worn out? Burned out on religion? Come to me. Get away with me and you'll recover your life. I'll show you how to take a real rest. Walk with me and work with me—watch how I do it. Learn the unforced rhythms of grace. I won't lay anything heavy or ill-fitting on you. Keep company with me and you'll learn to live freely and lightly."

The apostle John got this, and that is pretty much what he said in 1 John 5:2–4 (NLT): "We know we love God's children if we love God and obey his commandments. Loving God means keeping his commandments, and his commandments are *not burdensome*. For every child of God defeats this evil world, and we achieve this victory through our faith."

You're also going to notice that you fall in love with others. As you start this gratitude practice from the thankfulness chapter, you're going to fall in love with others in your life for whom you're thankful, maybe your spouse, though perhaps your relationship has grown cold over the years. God can turn that around, and it is his will to do so. You're going to learn to appreciate loved ones again—the people in your life you sometimes take for granted. You're going to love like he loves because you're going to become more like him every day.

We really can be empowered to do anything, I believe. Just look around. He made an extravagant planet for you. He formed a body for you. He made you his masterpiece. He gave his son for you. He sent his Spirit to help you. He gave his Word to speak to you and to guide you. He established a church to support you and he has prepared Heaven to reward you. He wants you to be there with him for eternity, says 1 Timothy 2:3–4. He wants the best possible life for you now, says John 10:10. He has incredible dreams for you, we find in Ephesians 2:10. He will *always* come to help you, according to James 4:1–3 and Hebrews 13:5–6.

Not only that but your self-discipline, like your muscles, will grow and become stronger. That makes it easier to do this every day. Is it going to be easy to start with? No, but as you go through it, it will become easier because you're going to see results, including increased self-discipline. I hope you're as excited about the results that are coming your way as I am! Another result will be Unity, the *U* in FRUIT. We'll dive into that in the next chapter.

Chapter 10 Bonus

Since we are talking about results, now is a good time to repeat the Personal Assessment you took as you started the process. Then compare your score to see if you are getting results. (*http://www.the100xlife.com/soiltest*)

Chapter 11—Unity

Another of the FRUITs that will result from this harvest is unity—unity with God and with others: our leadership team at work, our coworkers, our family members and friends. Why? Because we're not going to be offended by everyone and everything. Let's look closer at this unity. Unity with God. You see, God wants our first fruits. We read that in the Old Testament where he's asking for the first fruits, but he wants not only the first fruits of our wealth, but he wants the first fruits of our time—to be our priority. Giving that to him every day will create incredible unity with him in your life as you humbly submit to his authority, to his Word, and to what he's saying to you.

Walking in step with him is paramount. One of my favorite verses in all the Bible is 1 John 1:7 (NLT). It says, "But if we are living in the light, as God is in the light, then we have fellowship with each other, and the blood of Jesus, his Son, cleanses us from all sin." Another version says, "If we are walking in the light." Notice this "cleanses" is in the present progressive tense; it is ongoing. This is a great comfort to me, you see, because I know I'm going to continue to sin. I'm not perfect, you're not perfect, and the fact that he continues to cleanse us of that is of great comfort and freedom. Also, we have unity with God because he already knows our heart and our mind. Working this system will unlock his will for your life, your purpose, and your gifts.

Romans 12:2 says to let God transform you into a new person by changing the way you think. **Then you will learn to know God's will for you, which is good and pleasing and perfect**. Because of this unity, you're going to seek ways to glorify him. Then that will become your decision filter (1 Corinthians 10:31).

Who else will we be in unity with? Number one is with God. Next is our spouse.

There's a really sad story in the Bible. It's a case of a man not listening to his spouse. While if he had listened to her, it wouldn't have changed history, it could have changed this man's legacy.

The man was Pilate. In Matthew 27, verse 19 (NLT), it says, "Just then, as Pilate was sitting on the judgment-seat, his wife sent him this message: 'Leave that innocent man alone. I suffered through a terrible nightmare about him last night.'" That's very interesting to me. When we read the story of Jesus' last days and his trial and crucifixion, we often skip over this part. One morning I was reading that and it just hit me: Pilate didn't listen to his spouse. He was more concerned about what the public thought about him. He was more worried about what other people thought than about what his spouse said. She said to leave Jesus alone. My worst financial mistakes have all been when I didn't listen to my wife. I let my ego go ahead of what she felt, what she thought.

There's an interesting story along the same lines in the book *EntreLeadership* by Dave Ramsey. He talks about his wife and making decisions with her, in unity with her, and that if she ever gets one of these feeeeeeelings (with a drawn-out *E* because they're from the South like I am), he knows not to do the deal. There's a lot of wisdom in that, and I've since learned to do the same thing with my wife. You and your spouse were meant to become one. As you go through this process, as you realize whose you are, you will have more unity with your spouse.

We will have more unity with our children. Colossians 3 is what I like to call the "dealing with people chapter." In fact, in my next book, *100 X Business*, I'm going to feature that chapter along with some others about how to run your business according to biblical principles. In Colossians 3 (ESV), we read verse 21. It says, "Fathers, do not provoke your children lest they become discouraged." If you're going through this daily process of being thankful, being grateful, understanding that you're a child of God, and what that looks and feels like, you're going to understand that your children make mistakes just like you do. Yes, they frustrate you. We frustrate God. You're going to have more unity with your family.

We can have more unity with others in our personal lives. You're not going to be so easily offended. There is such a thing as mercy and we're told that those who give mercy will be shown mercy. Those who don't give mercy are not going to be shown mercy. Micah 6:8 (NLT) tells us what God requires is for us to do right, love mercy, and walk humbly with our God. Do the next right thing. If you messed up on that yesterday, ask forgiveness and keep moving forward, and be thankful you're still here to do those things. Show love to all people, even when they screw up. Be humbly confident in a better future and the greater power that is inside of you.

We're going to become more forgiving because we realize that there's only one perfect one, and that is Jesus, and we're thankful for that grace and forgiveness we've been given, so we can offer that to others. We're going to be more at peace with others because we're not going to be so offended and we're going to be more open and honest with people. We will be humble. Knowing that we're not perfect opens up a lot of doors for us to be in unity with others.

More unity at work is also possible. Make this a priority in your life if you're a leader or business owner. The business system I teach is all about this. We work to make your organization a healthy, cohesive team, with 100% of your team sharing your vision and executing on it day in and day out. That's when your business becomes fun. You really get to enjoy your company and you can get what you want from it. It can happen no matter the industry.

Who else can we be in unity with? How about your church family? I've learned that no church has it 100% right because churches are made up of people, and people are flawed. When you understand that, you can have more unity with your church family. What about extended family? We all have black sheep. We all have conflicts, but when you're in tune with God, you can have more unity with your extended family. How about friends? How about neighbors, coworkers, and even your customers? You can be more united with anyone in your community, especially those in need.

Instead of looking at needy people as a disgrace and as a burden, you may look at them in a different light after you've gone through this process and your whole outlook and filter have changed. No longer are you looking at them as a burden to society, but you're looking at them as a created child of God just like you, who perhaps hasn't had that opportunity that you have had, or maybe they made some mistakes. Knowing that you could easily be right there where they are, you'll reach out to help them.

That's it for unity. We're going to move on to the next powerful FRUIT of this harvest: *I* for Impact.

Chapter 12—Impact

"Each tree is recognized by its own fruit. People do not pick figs from thornbushes, or grapes from briers. A good man brings good things out of the good stored up in his heart, and an evil man brings evil things out of the evil stored up in his heart. For the mouth speaks what the heart is full of" Luke 6:44–45.

As a result of this daily process, you're going to naturally start to make an impact. Why? It's the law of reaping what you sow. When you put something good and positive into your body, your mind, and your spirit every day, positive behaviors and thoughts and actions are going to come back out. You reap what you sow. The Bible says, "From the heart, the mouth speaks." Jesus said each tree is recognized by its own fruit.

John Maxwell said this is absolutely 100% true. He was asked one time, "How did you come up with this speech?" after being asked to speak on short notice. His answer was, "I've been working on it my whole life." He's been putting in good material, reading his Bible, reading books. He's been working on it all of his life, this daily process of growth. It's the same thing. It's going to impact the way you talk. It's also going to make an impact on the way you look and feel. That is a reality. You have to walk the talk. People will notice.

There's an elevator principle John Maxwell also talks about, meaning you either lift people up or you bring them down. There's no in the middle. Too much of my life, I was a downer. Now my goal is to become an elevator, to lift people up. You are going to impact people by the way you act, and that's going to give you opportunities to share your faith. Then you can step back and let the Holy Spirit take over. That's a lot of fun. Different people have different gifts. I'm not naturally a big evangelist. I want my walk to share my faith. I'm not one who's typically going to go up to a stranger, and I'm not one to be yelling on the street corner, "You're going to hell if you don't repent tonight!" By the way, do you think that works these days? Yeah, I don't, either. I want my walk to show my faith. In Mark chapter 16 verse 15, Jesus said to his followers, "Go everywhere in the world and tell the good news to everyone."

I used to think that meant to go out into the world. I like the NCV version, which says, "Go everywhere in the world." The original meaning of that is, as you're going out in the world, tell the good news to everyone. Second Corinthians 5:20 (NLT) says, "We are Christ's ambassadors. God is making his appeal through us." Once you become saved, you go through the process of sanctification (becoming more like Jesus), this daily process of learning more about him. I am nothing more than "Jesus in a Stephen suit." That's who I am: an ambassador for Christ. Colossians chapter 4, verse 5 and 6 says, "Be wise in the way you act toward outsiders, making the most of every opportunity. Let your conversation always be full of grace, seasoned with salt, that you may know how to answer everyone."

That's easier said than done, and it only happens if you have these daily habits where this can naturally come out. When I launch the group challenge, we're going to work on delivering our natural strengths, our spiritual gifts, and then we will work to strengthen them further. I'm a big believer in strengthening your strengths, working on your strengths first, then your weaknesses. This is where we can have a lot of impact. Let me ask you a question. Is it nice to meet someone who is always full of joy, love, peace, patience, kindness, goodness; someone who's cool, calm, and collected no matter what's going on around them? Is that attractive to be around?

How about somebody who looks good because they look like they're in good shape, their clothes fit them well, they are full of energy and enthusiasm for life? Can we agree that those are the characteristics that are attractive to us? Those are what give you the opportunity to make an impact on someone who will look at you and say, "I want what they have. What is it about them? I want to know."

Then you're able to share that with them, as I'm doing with you through this book.

Realizing that you are a victorious, eternal, spiritual being just here temporarily on earth will give you more boldness, more courage to make a difference today. Now will you be scared? Maybe. Are you prepared? Maybe. I believe, like getting married or having a child, you're never fully prepared for those opportunities that come in front of you. Every day, doing this process, this system, God is preparing you more and more. I take great comfort in what Paul said in 1 Corinthians 2, verses 1 through 5, in The Message version. He said, "You'll remember, friends, that when I first came to you to let you in on God's master stroke, I didn't try to impress you with polished speeches and the latest philosophy. I deliberately kept it plain and simple. First Jesus and who he is, then Jesus and what he did: Jesus crucified. I was unsure of how to go about this and I felt totally inadequate.

"I was scared to death if you want the truth of it, so nothing I said could have impressed you or anyone else. But the message came through anyway. God's spirit and God's power did it, which made it clear that your life of faith is a response to God's power, not to some fancy mental or emotional footwork by me or anyone else." (Remember, this is Paul talking—the great Apostle Paul, who wrote so much of the New Testament—feeling inadequate.) How exciting is that? Pressure is not on us. We just have to do this every day and let the FRUIT come out to make an impact.

You'll also be able to use your status to impact others. If you're a leader of a business or organization, you are impacting others. They are watching you and you're impacting them for good or for bad. You're either elevating them or bringing them down. How can you use this status you have to impact others? By giving. You can't do this daily gratitude practice and daily time with God without becoming grateful. As a result, you're going to give. You're going to give more once you understand that. That's going to cause an impact.

You're also going to use your time to give back, to help others. You'll use your gifts and your strengths. That strength may be in your business. It may be in producing whatever you're producing to create wealth, and then you're able to give and help others. Maybe you're able to give more people work, to create jobs where people can be under you and be influenced by Christ living in you.

Then even your resources could be utilized. I encourage you to listen to my podcast episodes on first fruits (*http://www.stephenfskinner.com/first-fruits/*) and using your status for good (*http://www.stephenfskinner.com/036-use-your-position/*). Listen to Heartache for Hope (*http://www.stephenfskinner.com/episode-040-heartache-to-hope/*) for more information on making an impact. That's what it's all about: multiplying your impact. That's what the scripture of Luke 8 is talking about. Some produced even 100 times as much as what was planted. That is changing the world. That is bringing glory to our Father, bringing more people to Heaven with him. Let's go make an impact! Next, we'll finish out what this FRUIT is with *T*, and that's Transformation, the ultimate result of the daily process.

Chapter 13—Transformation

*"Do not conform to the pattern of this world, but be **transformed** by the renewing of your mind. Then you will be able to test and approve what God's will is—his good, pleasing, and perfect will"* Romans 12:2.

"Therefore, if anyone is in Christ, the new creation has come: The old has gone, the new is here!" 2 Corinthians 5:17.

"And Jesus grew in wisdom and stature, and in favor with God and man" Luke 2:52.

After going through this process on a day in, day out basis, of PLANTing, you can't avoid being renewed, refocused, restored, redeemed, refreshed, and rekindled daily. That passion you once had, which God put in you, will light up again. As a result, you will become transformed in your spirit, your body, and your mind.

How will you know when you've been transformed? One way is that others will notice, often even before you do. I started receiving messages and texts like this. This was from a friend I literally grew up with all through school, who now lives in Seattle. She said, "I love that verse you posted on Facebook. Your faith seems really important to you now and that makes me so curious about you. What happened, or has it always been that way? Something just seems really different!"

People will take notice and you'll start hearing those things. Your relationships will improve. You'll know that is a way you've been transformed, especially if you're the common denominator in bad relationships with your spouse, children, coworkers, and friends. They may not be perfect. You won't be perfect. I have a weakness with my tongue and text—a bad weakness. I still screw up, but my relationships have been improved. You know what I do now? I seek to restore relationships, which is another sign of transformation.

You will seek to restore relationships; you will attempt to reconcile with people you've hurt in the past. You'll be like John Maxwell was on the evening of his heart attack. He said he was lying in the hospital bed, going to have open-heart surgery the next day, and he really couldn't think of anyone that he had a conflict with. He felt a tremendous sense of peace knowing that if he died that next day, he was pretty much at peace with everyone that he knew of. That's a great place to be! That's where I want to be!

Below are other ways that you'll know you've been transformed. Most of these have been mentioned throughout the book, but it never hurts to recap:

- You will never feel alone. You're going to know that Jesus is right there beside you, in front of you, behind you; he's right there with you. You can take great comfort in that. You will know you've been transformed when you never feel alone, or lonely.

- Things that scared you before will no longer scare you.

- You'll look forward to your time with the lord. I can't tell you how many times I've laid my head down on my pillow at night, and I said, "Goodnight Lord. Thank you, I love you, and I can't wait to hear what you're going to tell me in the morning." Then I can fall asleep at peace.

- You will notice beauty more, in nature and in others; you will notice it everywhere.

- You're going to look better in your clothes. If you do this practice of nourishing your body, exercising, eating and living clean, then your clothes are going to look better.

- Your pictures will look better. Now despite my oncoming gray hair, if you see pictures of me now versus ten or fifteen years ago, you'll see I was getting rather chunky back then. Others will notice this in you as well.

- You will be prepared for the "suck" of life. As I mentioned, life is tough. There are still bad days. You know those days when nothing goes right. You just throw up your hands and laugh; it's just one of those days. You'll be prepared for that, and you'll be able to handle it, knowing that nothing you're facing is tougher than the exercise you did that morning, and also knowing where you're going to end up, and how you're on the winning team. You'll be prepared to deal with that, and you'll be at peace, knowing it's just not that big of a deal.
- You won't care as much about what you have or need. Cars, boats, houses—in fact, I have to admit I'm a little embarrassed with my house. I was a different person when I built it. As I mentioned in the last chapter about not listening to my wife, I'm not the same person now. I don't have to have that anymore. I'm thankful for it; we enjoy it, we love it, but it's not something that I care as much about having.
- You'll be more thankful for those things that you do have.
- You can hang with your kids. My son, who is an aspiring quarterback, thinks I'm the next Odell Beckham. I can get out in the yard and I can catch his passes, I can run his routes, I can keep going, and I can hang with him. I can play volleyball or tennis with my oldest daughter, and I can do cheer stunts and jump on the trampoline with my youngest daughter. Oh yeah, I can embarrass them as well, by doing my "Michael Jackson" dance in front of their friends! That's from the daily exercise, taking care of my body. We went on a youth group tour this past summer and we started this one particular song where we would squat down low and get back up. I would hear some of them talk about how tired they were getting. I

wasn't getting tired, and I'm in my mid-forties! Hey, you can hang with the kids, and that's a great feeling!

- You speak *life* into people. Instead of criticizing, slandering, complaining, or gossiping, you're speaking life into people. Instead of being a downer, you're being an elevator.

- People will feel bolder and more courageous after being around you. You'll have people who have been under you who will go and start their own business, start their own ventures, start to believe in themselves, and try new things because of your encouragement. That's how you know you've been transformed.

- Business will become more fun because the meaning of "It's just business" will be completely flipped. Whereas you used to say, "It's just business," meaning you were going to really cut someone's throat, or do something hardcore or unethical, now it means it's just business, it's not yours, it's what God's blessed you with, he's letting you steward it, and there are a lot more important things out there, such as the people around you.

- You'll be able to turn it all off at home, and become more present.

- You will care more about your people, and you're going to want to help them. Instead of taking them for granted as people who are there to serve you, you're going to follow the superlative example of Jesus, the unparalleled leader, and be a servant leader.

- You will listen more and speak less. That's a tough one for me, but I'm learning.

- You will see your interactions with people—customers, vendors, and everyone you come in contact with—as ministry opportunities, and you will seek ways you can add value to them versus finding out what they can do for you.

- You will notice acid reflux, or headaches, or hemorrhoids decreasing or disappearing, among other nagging health conditions you've been dealing with. You'll notice that those can go away. A lot of those are a result of lifestyle, and when that changes for the better, they may naturally go away.

- You will continue to hit personal bests (PBs), even after forty. They may be in your workouts, in walking at the amusement park, or even in your productivity in your sales for your company. You're going to hit PB's. Or how about even in your intimacy—you may hit some PB's there as well.

- You will sleep better.

- You may take fewer medications, but you may still be taking more pills. The difference is that they will be supplements, which are generally free of side effects, versus other medications you were taking that could turn you green and make your liver fall out. Remember, I'm a pharmacist—I know these things.

- You will know more about your field, or another area you've been interested in, which has brought you more opportunities. Anyone who knows me knows I'm a big fan of diversification. It's great to have different interests, different streams of income, and because of this daily practice of learning and having your mind clear, you're going to either excel in your field or find new adventures and opportunities out there.

- On that same note, you're going to see more opportunities everywhere. Since I started this process, numerous opportunities have presented themselves. This world has a tremendous amount of opportunities. If you'll just keep your eyes open, and look and pray for them, God will bring them to you—both business opportunities and ministry opportunities.

- You may fall in love with coffee, unsweetened tea, salads, juicing, and even exercise!
- You may fall in love with your spouse again or in deeper love with your spouse.
- Most important, you will fall in love with Jesus. As I shared earlier, I knew Jesus, and I knew he loved me, but I always thought his dad was mad, and I didn't really understand the concept of his love. It wasn't until one night after a few months of this daily process that I lay down one night, and I said, "I love you." I had never done that before. It was an amazing feeling.

Okay, you get it. Here, in my opinion, is the litmus test, and the ultimate way you will know you've been transformed. You will have more of these—you won't be perfect, but you'll have more of these. What are they? Here's the list:

- Love
- Joy
- Peace
- Patience
- Goodness
- Kindness
- Faithfulness
- Gentleness
- Self-control

Yes, that's right, those are the Fruit of the Spirit. Those will naturally come out in you. Also, you will not fear death. In fact, you will find yourself dreaming of Heaven, and you will have an eternal perspective of things, not a daily, earthly perspective. You're going

to feel awesome knowing you're on the winning team. I love
1 Corinthians15:55–57 (HSCB), where it says, "Death, where is your victory? Death, where is your sting? Now the sting of death is sin, and the power of sin is the law, let thanks be to God who gives us the victory through our lord Jesus Christ." You will know that, and you will be on that team, and you'll be so excited about that.

In the summer of 2015, I got a glimpse of Heaven. Where was I? I made a visit to Brooklyn Tabernacle. I was on a choir tour, and I had been told that the Brooklyn Tabernacle Choir is an amazing experience. I really wasn't prepared. There are some things that you're told about and it's not until you experience them yourself, in person, that you can really fathom them. This was one of those things. What was so marvelous is there were all races represented at this church, from all countries. I sat next to a man named Benedict. He was from Nigeria, had been living in London, and at the time of our trip, was an attorney in New York City. On my other side sat a couple from Jamaica and Antigua. Then when the service started, I heard the loudest praise I've ever heard coming from that choir, and they actually sang my favorite song at the time, "This is Amazing Grace," by Phil Wickham. I just wasn't prepared for that. It sounded like what I imagine the angels of Heaven sound like. All races, all people, and love, and unity, and praising God.

As one verse of the song says, "Worthy is the lamb who was slain! Worthy is the king who conquered the grave! Worthy is the lamb who was slain, worthy, worthy, worthy!" Yes! That's what I'm talking about! I wrote this in my journal the next morning: "I experienced a glimpse of Heaven on Earth yesterday. Brooklyn tabernacle, all races represented from all countries, the loudest praise I've ever heard, and so many people represented, all worshiping One God. The people were so kind, they would walk up and say, and "God bless you." It was amazing! I can't wait to see if that's what Heaven is like!"

Keep in mind that your transformation is not by your own doing. It does take effort on your part, but it's mainly from God. Every morning you will ask him to use you to bring more people to Heaven. This will become your focus, not the cares of the world, not the critics, not the ones who say, "You're weird now," or, "You're not cool anymore." You will be different, but remember, as Chris Hodges said, "You can only make a difference if you are different."

Finally, bringing others to Christ will become your focus regardless of your circumstances. "All these people died still believing what God has promised them. They did not receive what was promised, but they saw it all from a distance and welcomed it. They agreed that they were foreigners and nomads here on earth" (Hebrews 11:13 NLT). You see, this eternal perspective will lead you to the ultimate results: Eternal FRUIT—yes, the Harvest! Possibly, the 100X Harvest, Luke 8:8, which is what this whole book is about. Now let's celebrate that in the next chapter, as we conclude.

Chapter 14—The Harvest

"God's blessings follow you and await you at every turn: when you don't follow the advice of those who delight in wicked schemes, when you avoid sin's highway, when judgment and sarcasm beckon you but you refuse.
For you, the Eternal's Word is your happiness. It is your focus— from dusk to dawn.
You are like a tree, planted by flowing, cool streams of water that never run dry.
Your fruit ripens in its time; your leaves never fade or curl in the summer sun.
No matter what you do, you prosper" Psalm 1 (THE VOICE).

"By this my Father is glorified, that you bear much fruit and so prove to be my disciples" John 15:8 (ESV).

As I finish writing this book, we are approaching Thanksgiving Day, which is a great time of giving thanks and celebrating that originated with the celebration of the harvest, as did many festivals and traditions that we celebrate in the fall time of the year. Things such as Oktoberfest and square dancing come to mind. These festivals originate as far back as Exodus. In Exodus 23:16, it says, "Celebrate the Festival of the harvest with the first fruits of the crops you sow in the field."

Just like a crop, now we're beginning to see some growth. As you finish this book, sprouts and buds are beginning to emerge. The masterpiece that God created you to be for good works (Ephesians 2:10) is coming about. It's time to take a moment and reflect on where you started and where you are now. Maybe you're not as far along as you wanted to be, but that's okay. Just keep pushing play, keep showing up every morning.

James 5:7–8 says, "Be patient, then, brothers and sisters, until the Lord's coming. See how the farmer waits for the land to yield its valuable crop, patiently waiting for the Autumn and Spring rains. You too be patient and stand firm because the Lord's coming is near." In 2 Timothy 2:6, Paul is telling young Timothy, "A hardworking farmer should be the first to enjoy the fruit of their labor." Take time as you go along in this process and enjoy the journey. I hope I've made that clear to you. Go back and look at the chapter on being thankful.

Now, people go, "Look at you," as you start to be transformed. If good things happen to you, if you're blessed, they're going to say, "Boy, look at you. Look at how lucky you are." I want to remind you of the formula for luck that Darren Hardy wrote about in his book *The Compound Effect*. He said the complete formula for getting lucky is preparation (which is personal growth) plus attitude (which is your belief and mindset) plus opportunity (which is God's blessing) plus action (which is doing something about it) equals getting lucky.

Allow me to put that into these principles of this book. Preparation equals PLANT, plus attitude (faith, mindset of no matter what your circumstances are, [Philippians 4:13]), plus opportunity (a good thing coming your way or an opportunity to do good [Colossians 4:5]), plus action (Exodus 14:15), equals luck (John 10:10, Ephesians 3:20, Luke 8:8, Jeremiah 29:11, 1 Corinthians 2:9). Now, if you've gone through this book and you're not feeling this, you're not sure about it, evaluate how your soil is. As Jesus said, you're in one of four places.

1) You read this, but you are just not convinced this is the way of life for you. You think maybe you're not good enough. Your ground is hard. I want to let you know this is a lie from the Enemy. Go back and read it yourself, Luke 8:12.

2) You read this, you agree with it, and you're ready, and maybe you started, but you got sick, or you had a bad day, and now you want to give up. It's just not worth it. You, my friend, have rocky ground, Luke 8:13. This system is simple but it's not easy. You must **decide** and **commit** in order to **succeed**. You must keep pushing play!

3) You read this, you agree, and it sounds awesome, but you're just too busy and you're too tired to get up early in the morning. No one is as busy as you are. No one has to deal with the things and the people you have to deal with. You're overwhelmed. You feel like nothing can get you out of this mess. This is also a lie straight from hell. You just need to clear some thorns. This is a big American problem. Look at Luke 8:14.

The question I'll ask you again, as I asked earlier in the book, what if your largest prospect, your largest deal, or your largest customer wanted to meet with you tomorrow at 5:30 am for a breakfast meeting, would you do it? Think about that. Actually, I want to stress to you, when things get thorny is when you actually need to double down and focus more. Remember what Martin Luther said? He said he must spend an hour a day with the Lord first thing in the morning. When he had a busy day, he would spend two. Think about that.

4) You read this and you agree. In fact, you love it, and you are in no matter what! Congratulations, you are preparing your soil to become fertile and have a possible 100 times impact in harvest and all that we've discussed in this book that comes with it, Luke 8:15.

These are your choices. It's completely up to you. The system does work. I guarantee it. Is it because of me? No. It's because it's based on timeless principles and it's based on how we were created by our Creator.

This book is geared toward leaders, business owners, and entrepreneurs, but it works no matter your background, no matter your education level, and no matter your income. I believe I've shown that throughout the chapters. The cost is minimal. It does require time. Like I said, it requires effort. It's simple, but it does require some work. I do believe that if you read this book and you're not a leader, after going through this system for a time, the leader in you will emerge even though you may not be one now.

Is this important? Is it important to use this system? Look at what Jesus said in verse 8 of that same chapter, Luke 8. He says, "When he said this, he called out, 'Whoever has ears, let them hear!'" It says he called out. To me, this would mean that he shouted, he emphasized *pay attention to this*. The Message versions say, "Are you listening to this? Really listening?"

You add this formula of PLANT, plus rules of success that I learned from the strategic coach, Dan Sullivan, and it will equal success in life and business. I believe if you put these principles into practice along with those rules of success, you can really learn, start, and be successful in almost any business or venture you set out to achieve.

Am I guaranteeing success? No. We talked about that already. There may be failures along the way, although, remember, there is never a failure, there's just a chance to learn. When you have an eternal perspective that you should be grasping by now, a failure still won't change the fact that you are on the winning team.

What are those rules of success? There are four things. Add these to the PLANT process, and you should have success in whatever endeavor you pursue:

1. Show up on time.
2. Do what you say you'll do.
3. Finish what you start.
4. Say "please" and "thank you."

What kind of success? You may desire earthly success, to have a thriving business or more power. That may be what you think now, and that's fine. There is nothing wrong with success, but that's not true success. This is about 100 times impact for God's kingdom, not ours. Darren Hardy explains true success: "True achievement and life fulfillment is when you have success at home, in the marketplace, and with the triad of your being, body, mind, and spirit."

What is that true success? How do we know that we've achieved success? It's about your FRUIT. What is that fruit? Number one is eternal fruit. What is that? It is lives turned toward God. You're moving people closer to him. You're prompting yourself and others to do good deeds. Remember, you are a leader and leaders have influence, whether it's for good or bad. As a pastor friend of mine says, "Make his name famous." You give credit where credit is due. You acknowledge that you don't own anything, none of the success is from you, and everything is from him and him alone.

Further, there will be fruit which comes directly from his living in us. It's his fruit which is **the Fruit of the Spirit**. That's from Galatians 5:22–23. It says the Fruit of Spirit is: "Love, joy, peace, patience, kindness, goodness, faithfulness, gentleness, and self-control because against those things, there is no law." Once again, I ask, which is more appealing as a leader? Would you want to follow someone with those qualities or the opposite? Let's break them down briefly here.

- **Love:** This is servant leadership, the level-five leader Jim Collins mentions in his book, *Good to Great*. The superlative level-five leader is Jesus Christ. Love is meeting people's unmerited needs.
- **Joy:** To me, this is the secret sauce of what draws people to Christ. When they see joy in you no matter what the

circumstance is, when you display an inner happiness no matter what, they are intrigued.

- **Peace:** This means getting along with others no matter what and being content.
- **Patience:** This is trusting God, putting up with others even when we don't want to. It's trusting that God has a plan, though it may be taking longer than we would like it to take.
- **Kindness:** Kindness is acting on those thoughtful promptings. Have you seen the movie *Cinderella* that recently came out, the revised version from Disney? It had a saying that was repeated throughout the movie, "Have courage and be kind." What a great quote that is. That includes saying "please" and "thank you."
- **Goodness:** Goodness is being generous, giving of your money and also of your time. Money is nothing but influence in the world. I want you to make as much as possible so that he can be glorified, not you; but also, goodness is taking time to help people you know can't help you back.
- **Faithfulness:** This is being reliable, having integrity, being trustworthy, and knowing if you say you'll do something, others can count on it. That's doing what we say we'll do, and finishing what we'll start, mentioned in those rules of success. Faithfulness with God is showing up for your meeting every day with him. It will become easier over time. This almost becomes like a suckle of faith where it becomes easier and easier as you go along. In Hebrews 11:6, it says it's impossible to please God without faith. Anyone who wants to come in must believe God exists and that he rewards those who sincerely seek him.
- **Gentleness:** Gentleness is controlled strength or what I like to call quiet strength or meekness. I think of Tony Dungy and John Wooden as great examples of this. That's having humility, being humbly confident. It's having grace. It's

having your speech "seasoned with salt," and you're able to "speak the truth and love to others."

- **Self-control:** This is the self-discipline to push play every day even when you wake up tired and ticked off at the world. That's denying ourselves out of love for God and others. It's putting the greatest commandment into practice, which is to love God and love others (Matthew 22:37–38) out of willingness, not duty. That's calmness amidst turmoil. Like faithfulness, this becomes easier as we do it day in and day out, and it's the whole key to implementing this system.

Why do I repeat those so much, the Fruit of the Spirit? Why all of the reminders? Because it goes against our nature. In Galatians 5:17, it says, "For the flesh desires what is contrary to the Spirit, and the Spirit what is contrary to the flesh. They are in conflict with each other so that you are not to do whatever you want, but if you're led by the Spirit, you're not under the law."

"The acts of the flesh are obvious: sexual immorality, impurity, and debauchery, idolatry and witchcraft, hatred, discord, jealousy, fits of rage, selfish ambition, dissensions, factions, and envy, drunkenness, orgies, and the like. I warn you as I did before that those who live like this will not inherit the kingdom of God." That goes through verse 21. That's why we have to keep our eyes on the fruit, and let the fruit grow in us.

What do we do now? What do you do now? Where do we go from here?

1. **Never stop PLANTing** and harvesting every season. You see, if you lived off the land completely, what would you do? You would always have to be planting. Take this mindset in your life. Every 90 days, like the seasons, stop, take a day, take some time, and evaluate. Go through your journal that you started. Measure your harvest. Celebrate. Then, reestablish your goals for the quarter, the big rocks, and the things that move the needle in your

life. Even think about changing up your routine a little bit. You don't have to do it exactly, as I said. You may want to change from time to time as you go. Just never stop.

Why never stop? Galatians 6:7–10 says, "Don't be misled. You cannot mock the justice of God. You will always harvest what you plant. Those who live only to satisfy their own sinful nature will harvest decay and death from that sinful nature, but those who live to please the Spirit will harvest everlasting life in the Spirit." Let's not get tired of doing what's good. At just the right time, we will reap a harvest of blessing if we don't give up. Therefore, whenever we have the opportunity, we should do good to everyone, especially to those of the family of faith.

2. **Stay humble and thankful:** Yes, things are changing. You're feeling good. Perhaps you're even looking better. This fruit is being produced. Maybe God's blessing you like I mentioned. Don't get caught up in thinking that it's all about you. First Peter 5:5–7 says, "All of you, dress yourselves in humility as you relate to one another, for God opposes the proud but gives grace to the humble." Humble yourselves under the mighty power of God, and at the right time, he will lift you up in honor. Give all your worries and cares to God, for he cares about you.

3. **Armor up and stay alert:** Know that you have a challenge on your hands. Also, know this process will create a better world. Remember, this is a hundred times the impact. The Enemy doesn't want this. He wants you to make little or no impact. He wants you to stay where you are, to not grow, to not turn into that masterpiece that God created. We're told in 1 Peter 5:8 that we have an Enemy, and he's prowling around like a lion waiting to devour us.

I will remind you that in that same verse about the promise of the abundant life Jesus gave us, he also said there's an Enemy who wants to steal, kill, and destroy. John 10:10. The abundant life does not mean a stress-free life. You will experience setbacks. The sun is either going to wilt you or it's going to make you grow, depending on your roots and your soil. See Psalm 1 and Luke 8. You will screw up. You will get off track. You'll get knocked down. Although we're shooting for a hundred times, we're not perfect. Just remember, it's progress, not perfection. You're in a fight. You will get knocked down, but you must get back up.

You must realize this is not only for you, but you are responsible for those under you. You must fight for them. I have a wristband that I got at one of my son's football camps, and it says, "Passio Bellator," which is Latin for "suffering or passionate warrior." I look at that as my role as the leader of my family and my organizations, and I encourage you to do the same. You are a warrior for them. Ephesians 6:10 says be strong in the Lord and his mighty power. You must be strong for yourself, for your family, for your business, and ultimately for God.

How do we do this? How do we fight? The uniform. Like I said, you must do this. You must armor up. You must stay alert, and pray this daily or as often as you think about it. How about putting this on your mirror and reading it while you're getting dressed for the day? Think of it like your uniform. Jerry Rice, who is one of the greatest receivers in the history of the NFL, was obsessed with perfection, and one thing he was obsessed with was his uniform being perfect. It mattered to him. It matters to you.

What is that uniform? It is:

The belt of truth: from your time knowing God's Word, Ephesians 6:14. It's your shoulder pads, our rib protector of righteousness (verse 14). Whose righteousness, our own? No, it's God's. It's there to protect our heart. Put on your shoes of peace (verse 15) from the good news of knowing that you're already on the winning team because of Jesus and you can get others on our team at any time. So be ready, and know that no man can take that victory away. We can make the New York Yankees look like nothing! You know how they are notorious for spending tremendous amounts of money to get the best of the best? Similarly, we need to get more people on this winning team!

The shield of faith (verse 16). Let it grow stronger every day—stronger than even Captain America's. Captain America's shield is almost physically indestructible under normal conditions. Just like that is our faith, but we have to act on our faith or it will die. We're told in James 2:17, "In the same way, faith by itself, if it's not accompanied by action, is dead." Remember that. Interestingly, Captain America uses his shield both as protection and a weapon. Think about that. We can use it as protection, but do you serve a small god and big man or a big God and small man? Faith allows us to be bolder, and not fear man.

The helmet of salvation. As I've mentioned, my son loves football. He loves football helmets. He loves what's called the speed helmet, which is an improved helmet that looks cool to him, but it's been improved for protection. The helmet of salvation is verse 17. Unlike the football helmets that keep getting improved, this needs no improvement. Let me ask you, would you go out and play football against college athletes or NFL players without a helmet? No, it would be foolish to do that. You have no protection without salvation. You have no power. You must have this. His salvation needs no improvement. You can't earn it. You just have to accept that Jesus did it. You follow him and let him save you.

Finally, **the sword of the Spirit.** We hear the Word of God, that's true, but what about the power of the Spirit? There is power in his words. Once we're saved, we receive this incredible gift of the Spirit. Spend time and allow God's Spirit to fill you daily with his power from his Word, and from speaking to you through his Word. We have his Spirit of power in us, 2 Timothy 1:7.

Now, do you need all of this uniform? Yes, absolutely. What's interesting to me is we may forget this part: verse 13 says, "Put on every piece." You know what's also interesting about this scripture is it starts and ends with God's Word. He gave us his Word for a reason, and that's an incredible gift. I hope and pray that by now you see the immense value in using it. Wearing this armor and keeping our minds clear, we can resist the Enemy.

James 4:7 says, "Resist the devil and he will flee from you." Second Timothy 4:18 (NLT) says, "Yes, and the Lord will deliver me from every evil attack, and bring me safely into his heavenly kingdom. All glory to God forever and ever. Amen." Don't forget Psalm 91. Cut that out, put it on your door or your mirror, and pray that over yourself and those under you.

4. **Don't go at this alone:** We need a community. When Jesus was giving some of his last words to his disciples before he was killed, he talked many times about loving each other, and community, in John 13:34–35, John 15:12, and chapter 17. This is what he wants from us. God, himself, is a community. He is three persons in one, Father, Son, and the Holy Spirit. He sent us a helper so we would not have to be alone, says John 16:7.

   There's a great book called *The Enemies of Excellence: 7 Reasons Why We Sabotage Success* by Greg Salciccioli. In that, he sought to determine what causes leaders to fail. He has this cascading chart of the seven enemies of excellence that result in the likelihood of a leadership failure. Isolation is second to the top of the list. Proverbs 14:12 (NLT) says, "There's a path before each person that seems right, but it ends in death." We may think a path makes sense, but we can't see the danger someone else sees. They help us see that path.

   Also James 5:16 says, "Therefore confess your sins to each other and pray for each other so that you may be healed. The prayer of a righteous person is powerful and effective." This is why we need groups. This is why you need community to align yourself with like-minded people. Get in a church. Get in a small group. Maybe do a Bible study with your coworkers, your employees. Start one at work or with your friends, or I'd like to you to consider joining one of our group health transformation coaching programs.

Think about your spiritual gifts. Mine is encouraging, teaching, and leading. Mine is not singing. As we launch our online community, we are going to explore our spiritual gifts and our strengths. If God wanted us to be together, why would he create different gifts in us? He gave us these gifts to help each other (1 Corinthians 12). Ecclesiastes 4:9–11 says, "Two people are better off than one, for they can help each other succeed. If one person falls, the other can reach out and help, but someone who falls alone is in real trouble. Likewise, two people lying close together can keep each other warm, but how can one be warm alone?"

Why is it important that it's like-minded people? Second Corinthians 6:14 says, "Don't team up with those who are unbelievers. How can righteousness be a partner with wickedness? How can light live with darkness?" I think we've gotten this verse out of context a little bit, though. Some people think it means to not associate with any sinners. That's not what it's saying. It's saying not to make connections with them. You actually need to go out in the world, and associate, and tell others about the great news of Jesus, but they're not the ones that you want to lock arms with right now and do life together.

Other community inner circles are what we call masterminds. Being part of a round table is like having your own board of like-minded people. Although a church or a small group is great, oftentimes, I found that I was the only business owner or entrepreneur in the group. No one quite knows what you're going through—not even your spouse—except for other business owners. That's why it's so important to bring them together in a round table or a mastermind. You can find out more about the

masterminds and groups offered
at https://www.stephenfskinner.com/.

We talked about listening and talking to God but know also that God talks to us through others. Sometimes it can be an encouragement at the right time. Sometimes it may be a punch in the gut or a slap in the face about something you needed to see. Have you seen the Bob Newhart video (circling around on the internet) called Stop It? (*https://vimeo.com/10880189*) Sometimes we need that. We need someone to just say, "Stop it!" If you haven't seen it, you should go check it out.

We also need someone to coach and mentor us. The best athletes in the world have coaches. Look at professional golfers—they still have their coaches. We need coaches, but we also need someone to mentor. Look at the example of Paul and Timothy in the Bible. Mark Hall of Casting Crowns wrote a book called *Thrive*, which, by the way, was my go-to song during the writing of this book. It speaks so much to what this book is about. I encourage you to listen to it. He says in his book, "Just as God will use you as a Paul in someone's life, he'll also use your Timothys to help keep you focused on God and vibrant in the ministry. One feeds off the other, one helps the other, both love each other, all of it glorifies Jesus. That's community." Psalm 35:27 (NLT) says, "But give great joy to those who came to my defense. Let them continually say great is the Lord who delights in the blessing of his servant with peace."

The treasure, the secret of like-minded Christian business owners and the mastermind, comes about from this. It is a power of joining minds together, and then a third mind appears. What is that third mind? Listen to what Jesus said in Matthew 18:20. He said "Again, I say to you, if two of you agree on anything you ask for, it will be done for you by my Father in Heaven. For where there are two or three of you gathered in my name, there I am among them." That's the secret power that happens, and I've seen it while being part of different Christian business-owner masterminds. It's quite amazing to see. Consider joining mine. Visit *the100xlife.com/contact* for more information. If you've never seen the video called *Battle at Kruger Park*, I'd like you to watch it. The power of a mastermind group is like this video of wild beats versus lions.

5. **Finish strong:** Always keep planting. You don't have to follow my system, but you do need to make time to allow God to speak to you. Paul talked a lot about this. He was pretty adamant about this, and we must follow his example, and keep an internal focus on Heaven, not here (Colossians 3:2). This is an endurance race, and endurance races are not easy. If they were, everyone would be an ironman, wouldn't they?

   Hebrews 12:1 says, "Therefore, we are surrounded by a huge crowd of witnesses to the life of faith. Let us strip off every weight that slows us down, especially the sin that so easily trips us up, and let us run with endurance the race that God has set before us." I want you and me to race and finish like Paul. I want to run to win (1 Corinthians 9:24) by dropping all baggage and sin that slows us down so that we can run with endurance (Hebrews 12:1). We want to forget the past but look ahead to the finish line (Philippians 3:13), and press on to the end (Philippians 3:14). Then, we can say together we fought a great fight, we finished strong (2 Timothy 4:7). Now, we'll get to "Well done! Good job! That's my boy! That's my girl! Come on in! You've made me happy!" (Matthew 25:21). Now, go take your prize, your crown in Heaven! (Philippians 3:14, 2 Timothy 4:8).

   I'll leave you with the following parting thoughts and prayers. Why did I choose 100X? Because 100X will make you show up. Why is that? Because you're never going to get there, but, as we've talked about, quitting—retiring—is not an option. As we spend the rest of our days striving for that 100X impact, at the end, maybe we'll hear, "Well done. You impacted 50 people."

Maybe you will hear, "Well done. You impacted two." If that's all it is, that's great.

Luke says also in his book that when one sinner turns back, the angels in Heaven throw a party (Luke 15:7). I don't want you to ever stop, ever. Philippians 3:12–14 says, "Not that I've already attained this or I'm already perfect, but I press on to make it my own because Christ Jesus has made me his own. Brother, I do not consider that I've made it my own, but one thing I do, forgetting what lies behind and straining forward to what lies ahead, I press on toward the goal for the prize of the upper call of God in Christ Jesus." That's why we shoot for 100X.

I want you to flourish beyond your wildest dreams! Mark 4:8 says, "Some fell on good earth, and came up with a flourish producing a harvest exceeding his wildest dreams." First Corinthians 2:9 (ESV) says, "But it's written that no eye has seen nor ear heard, nor the heart of man imagined what God has prepared for those who love him." I want also for you, Ephesians 3:20 (ESV), "He is able to do far more abundantly than all we ask or think according to the power at work within us." The choice is yours and yours alone, but I highly recommend you *choose Life*! (Deuteronomy 30:19) This is my prayer for you: "Dear friend, I pray that you may enjoy good health and that all may go well with you even as your soul is getting along well" (3 John 2).

I'll end this book the way one of my mentors, Brian Hardin of the Daily Audio Bible, ends at the end of each year, from Numbers 6:24–26: "May the Lord bless you and protect you. May the Lord smile on you and be gracious to you. May the Lord show you his favor and give you his peace."

Next Steps

You may be thinking, "What do I do now?"

Take ACTION and START!

Here are some steps to help.

1. Join our private community on Facebook where I share a daily devotional as well as random health and wellness tips. Ask questions and get support!
https://www.facebook.com/groups/100xLifeCommunity/
2. Not on Facebook? I also post my daily devotionals on my website https://www.stephenfskinner.com/
3. Connect with me on Twitter or Linkedin. Just search StephenFSkinner on either one. I post links to my daily devotionals there, too!
4. Be on the lookout for my next book, *The Energetic Leader*!

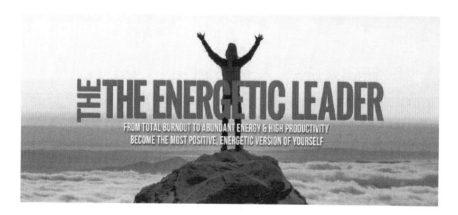

After several years of helping high achievers, I have determined that low energy has become a major underlying issue that is holding you back from being the leader you were meant to be, hurting your productivity, harming your health, and even causing burnout.

Low energy is an epidemic issue that results in low productivity and most of our health conditions. It causes us to not become all God has created us to be. Problem is, our culture and lifestyle are set up to cause us to fail here.

Over the years of working with helping leaders with their health, I've discovered 10 Enemies of Energy, which, when left unchecked, eventually lead us to live mediocre lives instead of the abundant life Jesus wants us to live (John 10:10).

Some of these killers are physical, some mental, some environmental, and some are spiritual.

I've learned how you can overcome each of them, and that is what my next book, *The Energetic Leader,* will be about.

If you needed more energy yesterday, and you don't want to wait to read the book, I have good news for you. I have an exclusive free online training for you.

In just about 45 minutes of your time, you can learn what these 10 Enemies are that are sabotaging your success and how to overcome them.

Just go to this page and you can get started today: https://the100xlife.com/10-enemies-of-energy-training

God Bless,

Stephen

Luke 8:8

About the Author

Stephen Skinner has been leading organizations most of his life. His first experience with leadership was involuntary: Within one month of graduating from pharmacy school in 1995, at the age of 23, Stephen's father expanded his own pharmacy business and placed Stephen into one of the pharmacies on the outskirts of their small Alabama community with a promise to be there often to assist Stephen. Due to the overwhelming success of the acquisitions, his father was not able to be there to help as he wanted, so for Stephen, it became a situation of sink or swim!

The author with John Maxwell—Stephen Skinner is a Certified John Maxwell Coach, Speaker, & Trainer.

Stephen's father started the family business in 1965, with a small community drug store. You know, the one on the corner that you had to go in to get that yucky pink stuff. He can still remember the smell and the sounds of "easy listening" music that always played in the background. In 1995, the elder Mr. Skinner expanded it to include two more locations and provided Stephen with the opportunity and challenge of a lifetime. The pharmacy became his launch pad, and over the next 20 years, he built on this modest base.

Over the years, he became known for his entrepreneurial spirit and innovation. He was honored with numerous awards over the years on a local, state, and national level. He invented an appetite suppressant lollipop that he shared at a national convention. It is now widely used by compounding pharmacists throughout the U.S.

Stephen Skinner has started numerous businesses and acquired several companies and commercial properties. He's grown from one 3,500 square-foot building to almost 80,000 square feet of medical, office, retail, and self-storage space. He grew his business to more than 15 employees and learned a great deal about leadership in the process, much of it by trial and error—lots of error.

In 2014, he sold his last retail venture to focus on his calling of helping other business owners like you, who may be where he once was.

Stephen Skinner's Contact Information

You can contact Stephen via email (*http://www.stephenfskinner.com/contact/*), connect with him on LinkedIn (*https://www.linkedin.com/in/stephenfskinner*), follow him on Twitter @StephenFSkinner, or like his page on Facebook (*https://www.facebook.com/SkinnerConsultingLLC/*).

Acknowledgments

Thank you, Ray Edwards, Jonathan Milligan, and Dennis McIntee. I'm very thankful to you for showing me how to write a book and pushing me to do this. This is something I've wanted to do for quite a while now. I always had that mentality that I wanted it to be perfect. I wanted the website to be perfect. I wanted to do this and that perfectly. I think that's part of my nature. You pushed me to go ahead and put this out there.

Thank you to my mentors and encouragers, some who know me, some who do not. You challenged, encouraged, listened, taught, and made me grow—either directly or indirectly. You have made a lasting impact.

Brian Hardin, John Maxwell, David Platt, Jerry Lawson, Matthew Hartsfield, Chris Hodges, John McKenzie, Randy Owens, Brenda Thompson, Buck Jacobs, Tom Rains, Dawn Owens, Ken Burnett, Aaron Walker, and Tom Schwab.

Thank you, Jake, for making me get out and walk. God worked through you to make me change my ways. We miss you! I'm sure you are loving your daily walks up there! Tell Jesus and everyone up there, "Hey!"

Thank you, Dorothy Skinner (Grandma) for being the greatest example of the Fruit of the Spirit (especially Joy), of anyone I know.

Thank you, Jennifer and Susan, my sisters, for putting up with me and helping me get back in line when I needed it!

Thank you, Mom, for your example of ageless beauty and the importance of taking care of yourself so you can take care of others.

Thank you, Dad, the greatest man I've ever known. Your work ethic, vision, selflessness, and unbelievable resistance to complaining or ever speaking badly of anyone make you, unlike any other person I've known. Thanks for giving me a chance, for making me sink or swim. Learning "Real Pharmacy" from you, and developing real estate with you have been a blast! Thanks for modeling servant leadership, and what our Father in Heaven looks like.

Thank you, Lauren, Ryan, and Lindsey! I can't believe God gave me you! You have taught me so much! Your love for Jesus and others is inspiring. You have made me a better man and are a large part of why I took the leap out of pharmacy ownership. I love being around you and watching you grow.

Thank you, Julie, my wife. Yes, I realize I "outkicked my coverage" more and more every day! I really don't know how I got you. Thank you for listening to the countless times I threw up all my problems at work on you, or asked you, "What do you think about this idea? You are the most amazing, honest, and selfless person I know. Oh, and you are smoking hot!!!

Thank you, Ruth and Lew Molnar, for taking a chance on a redneck Southern boy and allowing him to marry your fine daughter!

Finally, thank you, Jesus, for not stopping coming after me. I was running, but the more I ran from you, the more I ran to you. Funny how that works. I am so thankful you love us so much that you *never stop* pursuing us.

Contributors:

Jonathan Milligan, Dennis McIntee, my Amplify Group, my ISI Group, and Tom Schwab contributed input and feedback.

Jennifer Harshman and her team at *http://harshmanservices.com* edited and formatted this book.

Andrew Ledell at http://doneforyoutech.com/ created the website for the100xlife.com.

The JSH Group did the cover design through 99designs.com

Made in the USA
Columbia, SC
24 April 2022

59268369R10100